Leadership's Greatest Hits:
THE ULTIMATE COLLECTION OF LEADERSHIP LESSONS

Anne Bakker • David D. Coleman • Stephen Gray • René Hicks
Will Keim Ph.D. • Judson Laipply • Mary Lucas
Joe Martin • Curtis Zimmerman

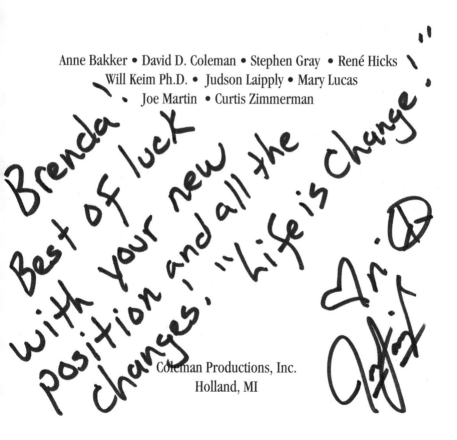

Coleman Productions, Inc.
Holland, MI

Brenda!

Best of luck
with your new
position and all the
things...

ISBN: 0-9743364-0-8

Bulk rate discounted purchasing is available by contacting the publishing coordinator listed below.

Published and Distributed by:
Coleman Productions, Inc.
402 Fairhill Ct.
Holland, MI 49423
616-392-8943
www.colemanproductions.com

Edited by:
Derek Emerson
Hat Trick Freelance
520 College Avenue
Holland, MI 49423

Cover Design and Layout:
abg design • Holland, MI

This book is dedicated to all of the people who have taught each of us the ultimate leadership lessons and made us a part of their lives, as well as to the schools, companies and groups who have provided the "CD player" to play our "Greatest Hits" on.

Tracks:

Introduction
By Barry McKinney

"So no one ever told you life was going to be this way…"

Immediately, your mind probably just added four distinct hand claps to carry on the Rembrant song, *I'll Be There For You.* Music impacts us in ways we never knew possible. Have you ever listened to the radio when a song makes you recall something or someone who is significant? You may recall a girlfriend, a boyfriend, a funeral, a wedding, or a special trip. Music can be significant in our lives because it creates the score and soundtrack. Just imagine some of our great movies without a musical score or soundtrack. Disney learned that their animated features are received better and are more successful with a musical score and meaningful soundtrack. In fact, good movie music directors are so intentional in their use of music they can manipulate the audience's feelings and emotions to better appreciate the art form.

When your favorite artist releases their *"Greatest Hits,"* you may rush to the store to buy it. Of course their *"Greatest Hits"* has all the songs that have been most successful; some entertainers possess so much talent their *"Greatest Hits"* consists of songs that were at the top of the charts. Other *"Greatest Hits"* compilations introduce a few new songs that inevitably become hits. Every musical artist who releases their *"Greatest Hits"* has to know they made an impact on the life of someone, possibly of many.

The collection of leadership lessons you are about to read is certainly worthy of the title, *Leadership's Greatest Hits—The Ultimate Collection of Leadership Lessons.* Each of the authors is accomplished in making an impact on the lives of people they come into contact with. Each has a unique and special story that makes him/her the person he/she is today. Those stories create the tracks in this *"Greatest Hits Collection."* The tracks are enriched by the harmonies of effective leadership skill development and interaction with others.

One of the greatest compliments you can give a musician is to share with him or her that their recorded performance is not nearly as good as their live performance. Each of the authors of this book would be pleased to hear that feedback as well. Even as wonderful as the written word is, it does not replace the real thing, live and in person. And this book, while excellent by all accounts, simply will not capture the essence of hearing any one of these individuals live and in person. Yet, just like our favorite radio stars, we must have something that will hold us over until we see or hear them again. This book certainly accomplishes this goal!

When I learned David Coleman and his colleagues were planning to publish a book about leadership, I was as excited as I was when my favorite entertainer released her Greatest Hits CD last year. When I was asked to write this forward, I stopped, had an existential experience, and agreed. Of course, the next thought that ran through my mind was how could I fully capture all I needed to capture to espouse opening thoughts to work by people I respect and admire. To see them in their capacities as lecturers is one thing, to be among them contributing to leadership is quite another. Quite simply, I knew I was going to struggle. I decided to try. I may have taken one or more attempts at it, but in the words of Curtis Zimmerman, "That's okay. Trying something challenging and failing puts you one step closer to success."

I have the fortune of working with college students every single day. I have interacted with some of our future's brightest individuals and as part of my job, I get to impact their leadership development. Because of this, I have not only experienced the impact of these individuals first hand, but I have seen their impact on others. Each time, the result is the same—a standing ovation and several college students who cannot stop talking about what they just heard. I have witnessed this phenomenon in the past, and it followed some great concerts. This is true for college students and others. When people begin talking about something and a dialogue forms, no one can predict the outcome.

As you read this collection of *"Great Leadership Hits,"* you will more than likely laugh, cry, learn something new about yourself and others, and you will experience the impact of stories that will make you realize that every person you meet can color your life. You will realize that dreams can become goals, and you will realize you have what it takes to lead. Sooner or later, you may be contributing to the tracks of leadership yourself. And, if you do not believe me, try it yourself. And, if you stumble along the way, "It's okay, you're one step closer to success."

Barry McKinney is the Assistant Director of Student Activities at Texas A&M-Kingsville. His duties among other things entail, advising student government, facilitating the university's leadership development for students, advising Greek life, administering the Javelina Mentor Program, and oversight for the over 120 student organizations.

Barry is an active member of the National Association of Campus Activities (NACA) and the National Association of Student Personnel Administrators (NASPA). He has presented nationally for both organizations. Barry has served on the Board of Directors of the Boys and Girls Club in Kingsville, Texas. He is a former Vice President and Board of Directors member of Big Brothers Big Sisters of the New River Valley, in Virginia.

David D. Coleman

David Coleman, known worldwide as The Dating Doctor™, has been named National Speaker of the Year nine times: six times by *Campus Activities Magazine* and three times by The National Association for Campus Activities. He is a highly sought after speaker, relationships coach, and retreat facilitator as well as president of Coleman Productions, Inc.

David received his Bachelor of Science Degree in Speech Pathology and Audiology ('83) and his Master of Arts Degree in College Student Personnel Administration ('85) from Bowling Green State University, OH. He is an author of six books. His most recent release *Making Relationships Matter: 9 Ways to Stay in Love for Life*, his video and CD are providing people with the necessary tools to create a foundation for healthier, more satisfying relationships.

David has been featured in such publications as *Us Weekly, Glamour, Mademoiselle, Cosmopolitan, The USA Today, The Wall Street Journal, The Chronicle of Higher Education, The Washington Post* and *The New York Times*. David has appeared on ABC, NBC, CBS, WGN, Fox and CNN as well as hundreds of radio and television stations nationwide. He is a regular guest on 104.5 WSNX in Grand Rapids, Michigan, Star 94 in Atlanta, Mix 105.1 in Orlando, and KLITE in Bakersfield, California. From his appearances on radio, TV, live and in print, David has impacted more than 5,000,000 people in all 50 states and Canada. Audience members at more than 2,000 college campuses, conferences, single's organizations, churches, corporations and marriage encounter groups nationwide have experienced his energetic and entertaining programs.

His popular website, **datingdoctor.com** receives in excess of one million hits annually, and provides straightforward, realistic relationship advice.

Making Leadership Matter
By David D. Coleman

Somehow, you acquired a copy of this book. Perhaps you won a free copy, bought one after hearing one of the authors speak, purchased your own, or borrowed a copy from a friend or family member. Maybe your class is using the book for group study, or you just happened to stumble across it and decided to see what was inside. No matter what course of action brought the book into your hands the more important question now is why are you reading it?

Why are you a leader?
No matter your reason for reading this book, make no mistake that by doing so you are learning something and putting yourself in a position to win, to enhance your skills, and be successful. Is your goal to make a difference or to be indifferent?

Take inventory of why you choose to be a leader and why you accept leadership positions. People assume and accept leadership positions for a myriad of reasons:

1. They have a "servant's heart" and feel compelled to do things for others.
2. They have an ego to feed and thrive upon the notoriety, perks, and power that positions of leadership often provide.
3. No one else would take the position and they won or assumed it through default.
4. They need something of perceived substance to list on their resume or to boast about.
5. They want to change lives, positively impact others, and make a real difference.
6. They are seeking to enhance their reputation.
7. Being a leader is a part of their family legacy. It is expected.
8. Leading is innate to them and they know no other way of living.

No matter which reasons are accurate for you, the bottom line is that you see leadership as important. If you are going to make leadership matter, in your life and in the lives of others, then from this point forward your attention must be focused on everyone but you. Real leaders have vision, yet focus on the needs of others. People in leadership for the wrong reasons focus on themselves. Jim Collins, author of the best selling book *Good to Great*, calls it the window and the mirror. Great leaders look in the mirror when there is a problem and out the window when it is time to give credit. This is the humble person's understanding of life and leadership.

The Value of Leadership

Whether or not you realize it, everything in your life holds some value to you. How much you truly value someone or something is measured by the impact it would have upon you if it were absent from your life forever. Several years ago this point was proven to me in an instant.

One Sunday morning in December 1997, my wife, two young daughters and I were securing the house and heading down to the car to drive to church. Until that morning I always had a fear of my phone ringing because I knew someday I would answer the phone and it would be someone calling to inform me that either my mother or father had died. I was very close with both of my parents as they had been exceptional role models for me over the course of my life. I had tried to prepare myself for my parent's death for years, but until it happens, you cannot measure the sense of loss you feel. My mother had been quite sick for years and her death was imminent, so when I heard my former neighbor's voice so sullen and somber I knew she was calling to tell me that mom had passed. I was wrong. My father had died overnight from a sudden heart attack. She was courageous enough to make a call that all knew would be devastating to me. I knew at that moment just how much I valued my father.

Surviving that phone call did not make me a leader, but the actions I took following that phone call showed the skills and courage my parents had instilled in me. In my mind I had two choices: sulk, feel sorry for myself, and place a burden upon my sisters, or step up and manage all the funeral arrangements that needed to be handled. I gathered my composure and handled the arrangements through my tears. You see, being a leader is not something a position gives you, it is something an event offers you. I was able to use my leadership skills at that time to help my family. Many others have done the same. The challenge lies in using those same leadership skills in a variety of events, and perhaps even seeking out challenges that let you serve as a leader.

What is your phone call? What is the hurdle you know you will eventually face in life that will define who and what you are? Are you prepared for that moment? Have you made leadership matter for you? Have you developed the skills and courage and an appreciation of value that will guide your thoughts and actions?

This book will help you think about those challenges, but more importantly, they will show you there is no easy way to be "a leader." You will be called to lead at sometime, and you likely have already been a leader in different ways. How will you make your leadership matter? That is the question to keep in front of you as you read this book, and as you face situations in life.

Favorite Tracks:
- Focus on others first.
- Show your enthusiasm for and appreciation of the people you are working with as well as their projects.
- Don't be afraid to move tables and chairs. Actions speak louder than words.
- Let others hear how talented you are from everyone BUT you.
- Remember that success cannot be bought. The person with the most money in their budget is not necessarily the best leader. It is a person who can do extraordinary things within limited resources that motivates others.

Joe A. Martin

Joe Martin is a nationally known speaker, respected university professor, author and educational consultant. Specializing in student and staff service and retention, Joe has presented for more then 500 associations, corporations, colleges and universities, helping hundreds of thousands of staff members, educators and students maximize their leadership potential.

He is Founder and President of Real World University. He is also a national award-winning speaker, author, and educational consultant. Joe has both a master's and bachelor's degree in communication and a doctorate in curriculum development.

In spite of being reared in one of the toughest inner-city ghettos in Miami, Florida, Joe started his first business at the age of 22 and his second at the age of 26. He also became the youngest, tenured-earning faculty member ever hired to teach at a state university in Florida at the age of 24.

Website: RWUniversity.com and newteachersuccess.com

The On Purpose Student Leader

by Joe A. Martin, Jr., Ed.D.

What kind of student leader are you? This chapter will talk about different types of leaders and help you learn to become an "on purpose" student leader.

The purpose of leadership isn't about position, power, or our level of persuasion. Purposeful leadership focuses on serving with our hearts, not our heads; it's about serving for the bigger purpose, not the bigger pay check; and it's about serving by example, not by exerting power. The key question we should all ask ourselves as leaders is, "Am I serving my organization or myself?"

"Not Like Most"
While most have decided to become part of the problem,
we have chosen to be part of the solution;

While most have questioned "Why"?,
we have dared to ask "Why Not"?;

While most have accepted defeat,
we have accepted the challenge to compete;

While most have focused on the obstacles,
we have focused on the openings;

While most have been overwhelmed by difficulties,
we have transformed them into opportunities;

While most have given up,
we have certainly not given in;

While most have resolved to talk,
we have resolved to take action;

While most have lost all hope,
we have remained hopeful;

While most are discouraged by the output,
we are encouraged by the possible outcome;

While most have forgotten from whence they came,
we haven't forgotten who brought us this far;

And while most wish they were like us,
we're thankful for not being like most.

Why Be Different?

I wrote that poem several years ago as a tribute to all the wonderful students I've had the privilege of teaching over the past decade — a career for which I'm very proud and grateful.

In fact, that poem was first inspired by a question I received from one of my favorite students. His name was Steve Langley. I was leaving to accept a teaching position at another university, and coupled with the fact that my speaking career keeps me on the road 75% of the time, Steve knew keeping in touch with me would be a challenge.

As he sat in my office for the very last time in "his" chair, I could tell Steve didn't want to say good-bye. Over the past year, we had numerous discussions about life, the future, the world, and other relevant matters. I had shared so much advice with Steve over the past year that he probably could have written a book. After promising to keep in touch, he asked me a question I would never forget.

"Professor Martin, I know you've taught us many things over the past few years as it relates to our success, not only as students, but as future leaders. However, I'm just curious, what advice has been the most useful to you as a leader?"

His question took me aback as I struggled to remember all of the advice I ever received and had given over the past three decades of my life. Never had anyone asked me to pick the "best" advice I've ever received. I must admit, the question stumped me. The pressure was intense, because I knew whatever I said to Steve at that particular moment, in all probability, would never be forgotten.

So, after taking a deep breath, and quickly remembering the most influential people in my life, I responded:

"To simply observe and watch what most people would do in a critical situation and then do the TOTAL opposite."

With an incredulous look on his face, Steve asked, "That's it?" — anticipating more.

And I responded, "yes," and explained, "Would you agree that the most successful people you know or have read about are also great leaders?" Steve nodded affirmatively.

"Well, let me ask you a few more questions…"
Do most people accept responsibility or make excuses?
Do most people take action or talk about taking action?
Do most people focus on the solutions or the problems?

I could see the light bulb suddenly turn on in Steve's head.

I continued, "Now, replace the word 'people' with 'great leaders'' and what do you get?"

Steve responded, "just the opposite response to those questions."

That's right. So I told Steve if he wanted to be great, he had to dare to be different. I promised him that if he dedicated his life to being different when faced with critical decisions, I could literally guarantee his success — whether as an influential Chief Executive Officer of a company or as an influential parent at home.

As a result of my conversation with Steve, I decided to write "Not Like Most" and dedicate the poem to ALL of my students. And that's exactly what this chapter on leadership is all about — YOU becoming a different type of leader...specifically speaking, one who focuses on the PURPOSE of leadership, not the problems, perks, or promises of leadership.

Just Accept It...You're Different!

As a student leader, you must first accept the fact that you're NOT like most. When you chose to become a student leader, you chose to set yourself apart from every other student on your campus. While most students choose to attend college with the sole purpose of graduating and getting a job, you chose to accept an additional responsibility, which was to improve the quality of life for students on your campus. You chose to impact the lives of others by becoming part of the solution, not the problem. In short, you chose to make a difference. If you chose to become a student leader for any other reason than that, you might want to reevaluate your decision.

Why is it so important to understand the role you chose? Because although you intended to make a difference on your campus, you probably never anticipated all the headaches that came along with the position.

For instance, you didn't know the position of leader entailed leading students who could be somewhat apathetic. You didn't know that most of your efforts on your campus would go unnoticed and unappreciated by your peers. You probably didn't know that poor program attendance would become the rule, instead of the exception. And you probably thought that all of your peers joined your organization for the same reasons you did – to make a difference. Wrong!

After reality set in, you probably ended up second guessing yourself, wondering if the responsibility was worth it. Well, I'm here to tell you emphatically, "YES, it was!" Although you may face many problems as a student leader, don't ever lose sight of your primary purpose – to serve your college and the students who attend it. Be encouraged my friend. It's in moments of crisis that a true leader's potential is tested and revealed. And this experience, called "student leadership," is part of your test.

The Gift of the Handkerchief
Even before you ever decided to become a student leader, you were blessed with a unique gift that you brought to the doorstep of your organization and your campus. To give you a visual image of this, and for the lack of a better metaphor, I'll just call your unique gift a "handkerchief."

This handkerchief sets you apart from every human being on the face of the planet. It's your unique talent, skill, and ability. It's your emotional signature you leave behind after you've accomplished a task. Your handkerchief cannot be copied or duplicated by others. You are the original. Your handkerchief is authentic. Knowing this fact should make you very proud and less critical and more respectful of other people's handkerchief.

Your handkerchief was given to you at birth—before your parents ever laid eyes on you. In fact, your parents were probably curious to find out what your unique gift was. Because, in actuality, it's their job to help you discover it and develop it.

Why would I call someone's gift a handkerchief? Because of the many things you can choose to do with it. Trust me, this will all make sense in a minute.

See, when you chose to join your student organization, you also had to make a choice on HOW you would USE your gift. The operative word here is "use." The purpose of leadership, as we said earlier, is to USE your gift to SERVE OTHERS. In a sense, you chose to be USED by your student organization. If that sounds a little harsh, just think of the alternative. If you're NOT being "used" by your organization, then that would imply that maybe you're "use-less." What a scary thought. I'd rather assume you're "use-full" than "use-less." Wouldn't you?

In fact, when you chose to become a student leader, the choice was quite simple, you could "use" your gift — I mean your handkerchief — to serve yourself OR to serve others.

Given, some leaders choose to try to extend their handkerchief options by "using" other people. Some even choose to be "under-used" or what we refer to as being underutilized. To "mis-use" your gift in these ways should be considered a crime, because as a result of these decisions, the students on our campuses usually end up becoming the victims.

How you USE your handkerchief is a choice you have to make every single day when you get up in the morning. You make that choice before every class, meeting, or student conference you attend. You make that choice before every event or program you plan, manage, or organize, and before every action you take as a leader, including how you choose to treat your members and the campus community.

Unfortunately, in my past ten years as an educator, I've seen a lot of student leaders, MOST of them do some questionable things with their handkerchiefs. Here are just a few of the choices student have at their disposal as a leader:

1. The Blindfold:
Some student leaders and other members join an organization with no confidence in their handkerchief (i.e., their unique gift). Their fear of failure paralyzes them and their organization. Because they wear their handkerchief over their eyes like a blindfold—afraid to take action, afraid to make mistakes, afraid to make tough decisions, and afraid to step up and become the type of leader they know they can be.

Here are some of the phrases that are characteristic of a "blindfold leader":

"I wish I was a better (name the talent, skill, or ability), then maybe I could be more effective."

"I know no one's going to show up at our event, because I can never get students to support our programs."

"Why don't you do it, you know you're a better (name the talent, skill, or ability) than I am?"

"I'm just a sophomore, no one's going to respect my decisions or ideas."

"I know it's probably the right thing to do for our organization, but if I do it, the members will hate me for it."

2. The Bandit:
These are the student leaders and members who ride into an organization and rob it like a scene from Ocean's Eleven. You know these type of leaders (or members) when you see them. They have their handkerchief wrapped over their noses and mouths and tied behind their heads like bank robbers — ready to leave your organization bankrupt of members and morale. If you listen carefully to what they say, bandits will literally shock you with some of their comments:

"If there's not going to be food, then I'm not going to the meeting!"

"Hey, where is the next national conference being held? Man, I got wasted at the last one."

"I'm the (name the position), I don't have to do that. That's your responsibility, not mine."

"Who cares what the administration thinks. I'd rather ask for forgiveness than permission."

"Why do we have to have all of these meetings? I have better things to do with my time."

Why do I depict this type of leader or member as a modern day thief? Because a thief is defined as any person who takes something without paying for it. Bandits leave both their organization and their members broke— emotionally, professionally, and financially.

3. The Blower
Would you believe that some student leaders and members will actually abuse their gift by blowing their nose in their handkerchiefs, or worse, wip-

ing their rear end with it? You may think that's a little gross, but just think about it for a second. I'm talking about the organizational member who walks around with a poor attitude to the point that other members avoid them like the plague. How they ever got elected or why they ever joined the organization, I will never know.

These type of people are probably the easiest to spot in an organization, because their attitudes are so obnoxious. After blowing their nose and wiping their butts with their handkerchiefs, it's easy to smell them and their "stinking attitudes" from a mile away.

Whenever you see a "blower," they always seem to be having a bad day. They whine and complain about everything like they were getting paid a salary for it. They don't walk around with a chip on their shoulder, they walk around with Mount Rushmore on their back.

4. The Bib

To this point, it has been fairly obvious to identify what's wrong with the previous three handkerchief users. One is walking around afraid of his or her own shadow; one is robbing others without a gun; and the other is stinking up the organization by making everyone else miserable.

However, this fourth group demands your undivided attention, because most of us (leaders and non-leaders alike) were taught to use our handkerchief in this particular way —to serve ourselves. I call this type of student leader or member the "bib wearer."

Unfortunately, our lessons of self-serving were picked up from well-intentioned, but mostly misinformed, people in our lives, including our parents, peers, professors, professionals, the public, and any other "p" word you can think of.

Most us were taught to tuck our handkerchiefs under our chins like a bib—and wait for others to SERVE US. Bib wearing leaders and members are the ones who joined the organization for the wrong reasons:

"...to network with others who could help me get a job when I graduate."

"...to impress potential employers during a job interview."

"...to make decisions that would make me look important and be praised by other people."

"...to socialize and meet new people on campus."

"...to add this experience to my resume."

"...to get (name the benefit)."

On the surface, there's really nothing wrong with this list of reasons for becoming a student leader and getting involved on campus. But upon deeper inspection, there are some obvious danger signs. Allow me to explain.

Those who wear bibs are those who are ready to eat (to be served). If every one in your student organization decided to use their gifts in this manner, then your entire organization is going to starve (or suffer), because no one eats (nothing happens) unless someone serves FIRST! Does that make sense?

In other words, no restaurant will ever pay a customer for "eating" at their establishment. The customer pays, because the customer is the one being served. That's the key. You "give" first, THEN you receive, not vice versa.

Remember what we said earlier, as a student leader, you're here to SERVE your campus, not to be served.

5. The Busboy/girl
Which brings us to the final and most important handkerchief option–the option to serve others. The "busboy/girl leader" or member realizes that the size of his or her tip is based on the quality of service that he or she delivers to others in the organization—in our case, our members.

Yes, the busboy/girl does not have a glamorous job, because he or she is usually found cleaning up after others in the organization. Even though, busboys/girls don't get a lot of the credit, all of the workers in the organization realize how important that person's position really is. The busboy/girl makes others in the organization look good and feel good about their jobs.

And isn't that the definition of a true leader? One who serves by assuming and accepting responsibility, and empowers others by giving and sharing the credit.

The great thing about being a busboy/girl is when all is said and done, he or she ironically receives all the things (and much more) that the "bib wearer" desired from the position:
- Better networking opportunities
- More job opportunities after graduation
- Respect from their peers and their campus
- Deeper and meaningful relationships with others
- A stronger resume
- Professional growth and development

Gut Check Time
So the question is, where is YOUR handkerchief? Think about it for a minute. Better yet, what would most of your members, students, and/or faculty advisor say?

Like John F. Kennedy said during his presidential inauguration (modified of course to make my point): "Do you usually look at what your student organization can do for you or do you look at what you can do for your organization?"

In addition to JFK's question...ask yourself the following questions:

"Do I usually work for the benefit of myself or the benefit of my members/ team?"

"Do I usually give just enough to get by or do I give more than expected?"

"Do I get more excited about going to group/organization meetings or missing them?"

"Does my leadership position usually feel like a blessing or a burden?"

"Do I serve with passion (in what I do) or with promises (I usually don't keep)?"

"Do I lead by example or excuses (i.e., do I practice what I preach)?"

"Do I usually brighten up a room when I enter it or when I leave it?"

In a nutshell, would your members and the campus community characterize you as a "blindfold member," "bandit," "blower," "bib wearer" or a "busboy/girl"?

As a student leader, only you know the answers to those questions. And they are definitely questions worth asking.

Whether we like it or not, we will ALL leave some type of "leadership legacy" on our campus. And that leadership legacy will usually consist of one of the following:

> A leader FOR the students!
> A leader FOR her/himself!
> A leader FOR-gotten!

A wise man once told me that "the best thing you can leave behind when you die is good impression." Well, it's my hope that the impression you leave on your campus AFTER you graduate from college is one of outstanding service to your organization and the campus community—the true purpose of leadership.

And if you are indeed remembered for being a servant leader, I can almost guarantee you, as I did Steve (my former student), you won't be like most. But more importantly, you will have made a difference because YOU were different.

Favorite Tracks:

- Consciously examine yourself and the position of your handkerchief before you start, attend, or conduct any meeting, program, or event. Evaluate yourself.

- Find another respected organization leader (or member) to find out where your handkerchief has been positioned. This should be done at least once a month (if not more).

- At the START of every week, ask yourself: What could I do to "serve" my organization better this week.

- Ask yourself this question at the END of every week: If everyone in my organization was just like me, would my advisor resign? If so, what do I need to change. If not, what am I doing right?

Curtis Zimmerman

Curtis Zimmerman is among the nation's premier speakers and entertainers. As an award-winning mime, juggler, and fire-eater, people have been dazzled by his unique ability to inspire. His secret is that he uses these skills to be one of the most inspirational speakers you'll ever encounter. Curtis sensitively balances the connection between education and entertainment while weaving together a highly interactive and life-changing message. He has presented thousands of lectures, performances, and workshops throughout the United States and abroad. He has appeared on every major television network and has been featured on numerous television programs.

A frequent consultant for corporations and educators, Curtis has received dozens of national and regional awards and fellowships. The Association for the Promotion of Campus Activities recently nominated him for Speaker of the Year. Curtis is the author of *I believe...what do you believe?* and coauthor of *Welcome to the Time of Your Life*. Curtis lives in Cincinnati, Ohio with his wife and two children.

Website: curtiszimmerman.com

To Motivate Others, You Must Be a LEADER

By Curtis Zimmerman

This chapter will provide a deeper understanding of what real leadership is and how a leader reacts to any given situation based on his beliefs, ethics, and knowledge. Empowered by this information, you will more adequately be able to make critical decisions and distinctions in your life, relationships, and work environment.

When people approach me about being a motivational speaker, they often ask: "Can you motivate me?" "How do you motivate a large crowd and get them to be better at what they do or don't do and change their habits and behaviors forever?"

My response is simple: I cannot motivate anyone to do or say anything they are not ready, willing and able to act upon themselves. However, I can share tools and true-life stories arising from my personal successes and failures that I hope will inspire people to believe more strongly in themselves and, therefore, lead them to action.

I consider myself to be just like a hypnotist. Anyone who knows anything about hypnosis realizes that a hypnotist has never actually "hypnotized" anyone. Rather, he deftly encourages us to take a journey with him to an even deeper state of consciousness more quickly than we could have arrived there on our own.

The same principles apply to motivational speaking. I do not attempt to tell anyone how to motivate themselves and others. Instead, I hand them a virtual mirror that will reflect the best person and leader they can be. Period.

If you remain 100 percent true to yourself, to your word, to your values and to your relationships, you can inspire yourself and others to reach levels of achievement you have not yet imagined. True motivation is really nothing more, nor less, than inspirational leadership.

Look for things other people overlook.

When we look for what makes a good leader—a good motivator—it is important we first realize there are as many types of leaders as there are factions of people. They usually play many different roles in various situations and don't need affirmation to know they are successful. They are more often the person in the grocery store standing next to you than the football coach, astronaut, or Marine Corps sergeant we tend to think of as stereotypical leaders.

The leaders I will describe in this article are ones who lead by example and who motivate people through their love, hard work, and patience. These leaders are just as demanding, driven, and powerful as some of the stereotypical leaders I previously mentioned, but they are not starry-eyed dreamers. They have an end product and timeline in mind. And believe it or not, they can be you.

An important point to remember in becoming a leader who is also a motivator is that it is an ongoing process. Begin by thinking of the people that are around you every day—family, friends, co-workers and classmates. These are the people you have the power to lead and influence each day by your actions, as well as by your reactions to what they say and do.

Experience the influence of a leader.

Envision someone you personally know who has leadership qualities. What is it they say and do on a daily basis that makes them a leader, that enables them to motivate others to action? Is it different from the way you respond to situations? Become a detective and watch this person closely. What habits, beliefs, standards, ethics, and power do they exhibit? How aware are they that others are watching?

A true leader/motivator will show you that having power is not as important as knowing when to put it into motion. Such a person knows when to speak, to remain silent, to act, to nurture, to challenge and to step back and allow others to take the lead. These are the skills of a true leader/motivator. Leadership is not founded on good management; it is the magic of interpersonal relationships and being driven to positively inspire others.

We have all experienced the influence of an inspiring leader in our past. My first experience with a real leader took place when I was twelve years old. I used to walk to a nearby shopping mall in Torrance, California, and play video games, watch people, and hang out with my friends. One Saturday afternoon, my life would be changed forever. I saw two mimes performing in the mall. They were doing a mechanical robot routine. I was mesmerized. That night all I could do was practice the mechanical robot. The next day I hurried back to the mall and yes, they were there again. I ended up following Tommy and Katie for five weeks. Everywhere they went in the mall, they had an admirer following them. (They call this stalking, now.) Finally, I got up all of my courage and went to speak to Tommy. I simply said, "I can do what you do!" Luckily for me, he was a real person. You know them as leaders. He said, "Well, let's see little man." I did my mechanical routine for him. He simply said, "Come back tomorrow." That night I could hardly sleep anticipating the next day's events. The following day was very different than all the other days I spent at the mall. Tommy had gathered some of the mall executives and the entertainment director together and told me, "Show them what you showed me yesterday." What happened next I did not know for several years. But here's what actually transpired. I did my robot routine and when I finished, they looked at Tommy and said, "So?" Tommy said, "I want you to hire him this summer and I will teach him and mentor him." With a laugh they replied, "Tommy you're one of the best mimes in all of Los Angeles. Why would we hire some kid off the street?" He simply stated, "Why? Because if you don't, I quit." "We have no budget," they replied, "be reasonable." Then, as only a real leader would react, Tommy said, "You'll pay him $5 an hour and take it out of my pay."

They threw their hands up, walked away, and he saved one life that day— my life. Every hour I worked, as he trained me, he made $5 an hour less and never told my mom, anyone, or me. That is true leadership. You have that power too, everyday.

Ask yourself the following questions about someone who has had a major motivational influence in your life:
Why did I allow them to impact my life?

How did they help me shape my behavior and my beliefs?

Why did I value their opinion of me, of themselves, and of others?

Why do we sometimes choose a poor role model?

This final question is crucial when you consider how you can become a motivating leader yourself, because bad role models are more prevalent than good ones. Why? Because there are many who ordain themselves as leaders whether or not anyone else necessarily agrees.

Of course, you can learn from bad role models as well. Why didn't they have a positive impact on your life? Why didn't their opinions matter? But you can only learn so much from what does not work. Instead, try to focus on a positive role model. Usually one role model will not do; since no one is perfect, we need to find *qualities* in people we admire and respect, and model those qualities. Maybe it is their drive, their honesty, their optimism, their character, or perhaps even their work ethic. After experiencing a leader's influence, we can find many different qualities to study, evaluate and ultimately incorporate into our own style. What is important to remember is this: Because you are modeling someone else's *leadership* skills does not mean you have to imitate every aspect of their personality, or even agree with their lifestyle choices or values. We see an example of this when a young adult finds a music group he or she "falls in love" with. The music is so great that he/she decides they love everything the band represents. If this band happens to drink on stage, is notorious for taking drugs, being obnoxious or obscene... well, you get the picture.

The big mistake for a person in this situation is to allow one or two aspects of a person's talent or presence, to override the fact that they should not model every aspect of their idol's life. However, most of us do this quite often with successful sports figures or celebrities. Many of these people accomplish great things, but that does not mean they are great people. We need to focus on their years of dedication, passion for what they love to do, and burning desire to succeed, for these are some of the things that have made them leaders and motivators in their field.

Allow yourself to fail and risk failure.

In your efforts to become a motivating leader, you will inevitably run into obstacles. Every great leader understands that failure is a key component to success. The statement: "Successful people have failed more than [people who might be thought of as] failures" is not only true, but also a simple test to use to ascertain if you are growing and challenging yourself in a given situation or task.

Once you have reached the point where you are successful at an activity every time you attempt it, you are only demonstrating what you already know. You are not challenging yourself to expand your abilities. You are not risking failure. Willingness to take risks and experience failure is what allows us to grow and be driven to improve.

I too have placed limitations on myself that have held me back from reaching the potential we all possess. I had been performing professionally for fifteen years: mime, juggling, fire eating, and magic. My juggling routine consisted of three balls to the song "Dueling Banjoes." I had tried and failed miserably to juggle five balls and had convinced myself that it was impossible for me. This friend of mine invited me to a juggling convention. I was never much of a "joiner" of clubs or associations, so this would be my first juggling convention. It was pretty much what you would expect: a large room filled with people juggling balls, knives, bowling balls, passing pins, unicycling, etc. But then it happened. Standing no more than three feet from me was a young boy no older than fourteen. He was your pretty typical looking kid—jeans, t-shirt hanging out, tennis shoes. He had this beautiful blue velvet bag. As he reached in and pulled out five shining new juggling balls, I thought to myself, "in your dreams, kid." But to my amazement, he stood right there and juggled five balls for what seemed like an eternity, never dropping one. When he stopped, he placed all five balls back in his bag and walked away as if nothing ever happened. Now keep in mind I had been juggling for fifteen years and he was only fourteen years old. I was dumbfounded. I knew that very second I had two choices. One, I could kill him. Two, I could reevaluate my self-imposed limitations. Needless to say, no one died that day. However, two days later, at four o'clock in the morning, my wife was awoken by me in the other room screaming, "I did it, I did it! I can juggle five balls!" Now juggling five balls is not only possible for me, but is something I can do consistently, all because I stopped saying, " I can't." I focused on the goal and said it was attainable.

Determine your goals and expectations.

In order to challenge yourself and make sure that you are continually improving, you must set goals— realistic expectations to use to begin your journey. The reason people set goals is simple: They work!

This process involves determining your personal desires for your future, and setting up measurable, attainable steps to show your progress. As an example, I encourage every new student to decide before attending their first class what their grade point average (GPA) for the year will be. Doing this prior to the beginning of classes gives them power over their future and allows them to evaluate how well they are moving toward their goal. They can make daily decisions and change their habits based on what they need to meet their goals. In short, setting goals and expectations motivates them to do well.

Examine your thoughts and habits.

The most effective way to become a good friend, family member, partner, strong motivator and ultimately a good leader can be summarized in one phrase:

"If you think about it…"
Too often most of us choose not to think about *it*, whatever *it* might be:
>What am I doing tonight?
>With whom am I sleeping?
>What am I eating?
>What am I drinking?
>How do I look?
>How do I feel?
>Do I care?
>Should I care?
>What is my future?
>What is my past?
>What is important to me?
>Do I believe in God?

Do I believe in me?
Can I believe in you?
What will happen to me when I die?
Why am I here?
Could I leave a positive mark on this world...?
We can all answer these questions successfully if only we choose to think about them.

Answering these questions involves self-examination, looking closely at our weaknesses and strengths in interpersonal relationships, our work habits, study habits and willingness to give our time and energy away for free. Yet many of us choose to shut down the inner voice that guides us towards these matters with alcohol, drugs, or even by escaping into television, cheap novels and gossip.

Just... think about it!

Real leadership should be your objective.
Real leadership takes being honest and "real" with yourself. This can be simultaneously one of the hardest and simplest things to do. All you have to do is listen to your inner self, acknowledge what you hear, and then act on it. We often choose to shut down this inner voice through our bad habits.

However, being a real person is exactly what leaders do. When you go to someone who is real with a problem, they treat your problem as if it was their own. When you go to someone who is real and ask for his or her opinion, you know you will get an honest answer.

These real people are around us more than we realize or acknowledge. They are mentors, co-workers, family members, teachers, students, bosses, and employees. The only way to tap into their power is to become real yourself. This can be scary at first, but the more you strive to become real and encourage others around you to do the same, the easier this process will become. I know many people want to read an article that gives them the 10 steps to becoming a motivating leader. "If you just do these 10 things, you will be a leader, people will admire you, look up to you, and listen to you." The fact is that it is only when you are being real, honest, loving, sincere and giving that you can receive admiration, respect and loyalty.

Leadership—being the kind of leader who motivates others to achieve their personal best—is an ongoing process that takes dedication and decision-making. However, it is by motivating others to reach their goals that leaders ultimately reach their own.

Here are some personal thoughts and philosophies of mine that you might use to motivate yourself in becoming a leader who motivates others.

- Be on time.
- Show up with enthusiasm instead of being shown up by others.
- Say what you mean and mean what you say.
- Don't be afraid to fail, and learn to fail successfully.
- Remember that image is nothing, but action is everything.
- Look in people's eyes when they talk.
- Live today like it is your last because one day you'll be right.
- Cast your show (life) wisely, as it's the only one you'll ever have.
- The vocabulary we use on a daily basis shows the world around us our intelligence, our values and our integrity.
- You are the only person that you will spend your entire life with, so you'd better like the company.
- How to motivate yourself: find out what you love.
- By living in the moment, you can change your life forever from this moment on.
- Understand that leaders don't see the positive in everything. Rather, they believe everything has possibilities.

Favorite Tracks:

- When we look for what makes a good leader—a good motivator— it is important that we first realize there are as many types of leaders as there are factions of people.

- A true leader/motivator will show you that having power is not as important as knowing when to put it into motion.

- One role model isn't enough; since no one is perfect, we need to find *qualities* in people we admire and respect and model those qualities.

- Willingness to take risks and experience failure is what allows us to grow and be driven to improve.

- The reason people set goals is simple: They work!

Dr. Will Keim

Will Keim has spoken to more students on more campuses about actualizing peak performance and leadership than anyone in our nation. His corporate clients include AT&T, IBM, State Farm Insurance, several state human resources and development organizations, and Delta Airlines. He is the author of *The Education of Character: Lessons for Beginners, Spirit Journey, Life after College, The Truth About College, The Tao of Christ, Wit and Wisdom, Welcome To The Time of Your Life, Fan Etiquette*, and is a contributing author to *Chicken Soup for the College Soul, Let Your Leadership Speak*, and *Greek Inspirations*. Named a Paul Harris Fellow by Rotary International, Dr. Keim was selected as the Outstanding Professor at Oregon State University for his teaching in the speech department. Dr. Keim in an NCAA recognized speaker on life skills issues and was selected as an outstanding young man of America by the US Jaycees. He holds the prestigious Jack L. Ans award from the Association of Fraternity Advisors and is the father of four. A member of Delta Upsilon International Fraternity, Dr. Keim is an Intercollegiate Chaplain for the Christian Church (Disciples of Christ). He is married to Donna Keim and lives in Corvallis, Oregon.

Website: willkeim.com

Leading from the Stands
How to Honor Your Team Without Dishonoring Yourself
by Dr. Will Keim

A Chapter On Civility

When I was a boy playing basketball and growing up in Los Angeles, we had John Wooden. We knew how to cut our hair because we wanted to play for him. We knew we had to take care of our feet because he said time and time again that this was very important. We banked the ball from the side because he taught his players to do it and we wanted to be like them. I left my junior prom early at South Hills High School because KTLA Channel 5 was running a tape delay of that night's Bruin conquest. It wasn't until late in my senior year that I realized Coach Wooden was not going to call because very few teams, especially his, were looking for a 6'2" center weighing 150 pounds with 8" vertical jumping ability.

Coach Wooden had class. He had style. He maintained a gentleman's demeanor through hundreds of victories, ten national championships, and the occasional and highly publicized losses. Years later I tell my children, "Bank that shot. Bank the ball when you shoot from an angle. Hit the square." The Keim children ask, "Why?" "Because," I respond, "Coach Wooden said so." "Who is he?" they asked, but only once. "Who is he? "He is . . ." I stop and pull an old card from my wallet, a card given to high school students in the '60's by the Southern California Gas Company with Coach John R. Wooden's picture and Pyramid of Success and the Seven Point Creed given to Coach when he was 12 years old by his father. Showing my children the card I finish my statement, "John Wooden is the man who understood the importance of sport and play in the development of one's character. He was a teacher who taught life and used the basketball court as his classroom. He graduated nearly every one of his players before they started keeping track, and he is the greatest coach that ever lived. He was a loyal husband and family man who once said, 'There are only three important things in life: Family, Faith, and Profession. And number two should be number one, but I think He understands.' He was a man of deep faith and character and a role model for many of us." JJ, my nine-year-old said, "Did you ever play for him Daddy?" Pausing to remember some thirty years ago, "Only in my dreams son. Only in my dreams."

* * * * *

There was a time in our society's life when there were figures of central validity like John Wooden who taught us all how to behave, to think before we acted, to be measured in our responses, and to treat our fellow human beings with dignity and respect. What has happened? How has a burning desire to win become the desire to burn? How has a field of dreams become a field of screams? If the athletic department is the front porch of the university and if professional sports serve as visual training grounds for young athletes, what are we to make of the increasing rudeness, lewdness, profane, and violent behavior increasingly associated with collegiate and professional sporting events? Leaders lead and now is the time for responsible students to step up and take back the stands that have been claimed by fanatics. Leaders are real fans.

A year ago, I sat in a Division I football stadium in California watching my alma mater play football against an excellent opponent. Sometime during the third quarter I quit watching and began to plan an escape from the stadium. My sixteen year-old daughter had been asked to bring "her beaver" over to 20 drunk fans next to us (our team's mascot is the Beaver, so you can see the quick and witty intellect of the drunk guys who verbally harassed her); my 11 year-old daughter had been asked, "What are you looking at you f____ little bitch?"; and my wife had heard the lemon aid line, "I could put a knife in your back Orange (our colors) and kill you and no one would care." Charming? Collegiate? Welcoming? Good Spirited? No. Frightening. Scary. Terrifying to the children and me. My daughter said, "Daddy, I thought this was a university?" After having beers thrown in our faces, flags ripped off our cars, a little pushing and shoving, and the "F" bomb dropped as a noun, verb, object, and adverb, we escaped to our car.

That day drives this chapter. We must create and resurrect Fan Etiquette. We can honor our teams without dishonoring ourselves. **Why?** Because university administrators, faculty, campus and city police are growing weary of riots, burnings, and paralyzing accidents that take any joy of competition away. **When?** Now. Before competitions become more of a liability than any insurance company is willing to take. **How?** Let me share a few ideas.

* * * * *

What The Real Fan Knows
The Real Fan knows that the purpose of attending an event is to ENJOY it, not to embarrass themselves or their TEAM. True fans know that the action is on the field or the court and they are INVOLVED and informed about the games, not ignorant and irate. Real Fans understand the power of QUIET as well as noise to create a competitive edge. Good fans stand UNITED behind their teams and do not upstage the athletes. Their EXCITEMENT is productive and empowers good play and rewards effort. Classy fans TALK to each other, never using profanity or abusive language on their opponents or their fans. They TREAT others as they would like to be treated, and real fans know when ENOUGH is enough. The Real Fan knows **ETIQUETTE.**

The Disney Example
Think of your ticket as the right to be in a stadium or arena. It is not a pass to abuse the folks who work there. Disney's ticket gives you the right to ride anything in the park. It is a privilege removed if bad language, abusive conduct, or drunken behavior occurs. Maybe this is one reason it is the happiest place on Earth . . . you don't have to deal with foul-mouthed fanatics.

The Buddy System
We have designated drivers. Why not game buddies who assist us in keeping our conduct appropriate?

The Out Of Line Hotline
I suggest that each college or university set up a hotline that can be dialed by any cell phone identifying a person or situation about to get out of control before it does explode and distract the fans from watching the event.

The H.I.T. Team
A campus wide Honor Intervention Team of peer educators and advisors who might stem a problem before it erupts by quietly asking the rowdy fan

to take control and mellow out. These folks could be seated throughout the stadium and identified by cool shirts or buttons.

It's Official
Barring any self-control by a crowd, officials must be given more power to encourage fans to remain on the sidelines or in the stands. Does someone have to die before we keep the players on the field and the fans in the stands, where they belong? Fans have not earned the right to be on the field through thousands of hours of practice. Only the student athletes deserve to be there. Warnings should lead to penalties, penalties eventually to points and points to forfeiture. The professional sports teams do not let fans on the field. There are a thousand good reasons for this.

The Mouth and The Buttocks
If you ever hear someone yell at you, "Hey, sit down and shut up," then there is a good chance you are using your mouth too much and not spending enough time on your bottom. Take their advice and have a seat.

And P.S.
If you ever yell at the opposing team's band or boo them, get help. You have issues. Really . . .what kind of person yells at a tuba player? Get a life! I heard a guy yell: "Cymbals suck." Wow!

*   *   *   *   *

It is not my goal to make every event like a church choir loft. But sportsmanship has taken a big hit recently and games, even for those of us who love sports, are becoming less fun, even threatening experiences. Practice Fan Etiquette and encourage your friends to do the same. After all, as President Teddy Roosevelt said, "The credit does not go to the critic in the stands but to the warrior in the arena." If your conduct takes attention away from the athletes, then make a change and let them have their moment of glorious competition. Honor your team without dishonoring yourself. Practice Fan Etiquette. —Respectfully submitted in honor of Coach John R. Wooden by Will Keim, Ph.D.

Favorite Tracks:
- Enjoy the event
- Team First
- Involve yourself in the event
- Quiet can be a powerful tool
- Unite with your team
- Excitement: create it, don't distract others
- Talk, do not yell, at others
- Treat others as you would like to be treated
- Enough: Know when enough is enough

FAN

E.T.I.Q.U.E.T.T.E.

René Hicks

René Hicks is not a medical doctor, although she says that one day she would like to play one on TV. However, as an internationally known comedian (2 Time NACA Comedian of the Year) she recognized very early in her career the healing power of laughter. Often categorized as a comic with a social conscience, René is determined to use her comedy to make a difference in people's lives. By addressing societal ills through humor and in the speaking area, she provides quality entertainment that makes people laugh, while also delivering a powerful message. That message is: Through laughter we can break down barriers that contribute to social isolation and intolerance.

René is taking her message on the speaking circuit, with an expanded concept of healing humor, developed after she recently survived a major health crisis—lung cancer. She found that her God-given gift for creating laughter was instrumental in helping her heal as well as helping those around her to cope with such an unexpected and uncertain life altering situation. René's passion is an example to others. Through her laugh-filled lecture on how to effectively enlist humor into our lives she drives home the point that laughter is an aid which can help us overcome major obstacles and upheavals in our lives.

René has performed in venues worldwide. She has appeared on numerous television shows including her own half hour special—***Comedy Central Presents...René Hicks***. René will have you Laughing...for the Heath of IT!

Laugh for the Health of It!

by René Hicks

Laughter is an amazing healing agent that when applied to everyday "cancers" in our lives can not only cure physical ailments but close the divides between people.

I am not a medical doctor, although one day I would like to play one on TV. Why? Because laughter heals! I already knew this, but some scientists were kind enough to agree with me. Laughter elevates mood, lowers blood pressure, and makes the immune system more robust. However, a disturbing trend emerges from the research. A child laughs on average 400 times each day. By the time that child reaches adolescence, it goes down to 200 times each day. By the time that child reaches undergraduate status, undergrads usually being the subjects at the end point of these studies, the rate has gone down to 18-20 times a day. I know what you sceptics are thinking. "Only 18-20 times a day, when did college students get so serious? Isn't college life looked back on as the most fun time of a person's existence?" Well, maybe they just included students majoring in accounting, economics and statistics in the study.

The good news is even a lay person can design a clinical intervention to improve our health by addressing the potential health crisis brought on by humor deficits. It's simple....Laugh for the Health of it! As a painless inoculation of humor in order to improve overall health I prescribe a healthy dose of laughter to be taken at least 500 times a day or more if needed.

You don't have to be a kid to laugh like one, although I do believe kids have a natural proclivity to use laughter as a cure all. I was five years old the first time that I can recall laughter and healing being associated together. It was while I spent months recuperating from third-degree burns that almost resulted in my early arrival at the big playground in the sky. Everyone—my family, doctors, nurses, etc., did any and everything possible to keep my spirits up through the painful and arduous healing process, and their success was often measured by my laughter. I can remember hearing comments like "Oh, she's laughing, she's going to be just fine." So, reasoning like a 5-year-old, I thought the more I laughed the quicker I would get to go home. That was the first time, unknowingly, that the importance of using humor in difficult times was successfully implemented in my life.

Perhaps it's because of this early brush with death that I have maintained a childlike ability to laugh when I could be crying. More importantly, I have always been able to use that ability to help others find how to effectively enlist humor in their own lives, as an aid in overcoming major obstacles and upheavals that everyone is bound to face in the course of a lifetime. Whether those obstacles and upheavals are of a life threatening nature or just life impeding, if you can find humor in a difficult situation, you're well on your way to finding an easier solution. They say that love is so powerful it can move mountains, but laughter is equally as powerful, because it will help cure your depression after you break up with the person you moved that mountain for in the first place!

My grandfather also instilled the power of laughter in me. My grandfather is one of the funniest people that I've ever met—profoundly funny. Born and raised in the segregated south, my grandfather's life philosophy was that " if you can't laugh at life, then check your pulse, you might be dead and if you're not dead, you might as well be." He taught me that historically oppressed people tend to distract themselves from the seemingly horrendous and hopeless conditions that surround them by using laughter. It was my grandfather who told me that the telling of the popular "yo mama" jokes, originally termed "Playing the Dozens," was a method devised by blacks in the "Jim Crow" south to anaesthetize black men against the taunts and insults, specifically with regard to their mothers, hurled at them by bigots. The natural inclination of any man would be to defend the honor of his mother, which in those times would have most assuredly provoked a harsh retaliation by those very same bigots, resulting in those black men being beaten or even lynched. So, black men would play a game of intentionally tossing back and forth the most stinging insults about each other's mothers. This proves laughter not only can heal, but it can actually keep people from getting killed. "Yo mama so ugly she could make an onion cry." "Yo mama so black that one night someone tried to shoot her, but the bullet had to come back and ask directions." "Yo mama so old that when Moses parted the Red Sea, she was on the other side fishing."

These brutal verbal attacks on each other's mamas was done so that when they heard bigots saying vile things against their mothers, it would not have the desired effect of making them angry, because they would have routinely heard far worst and laughed about it.

I've been truly ethereally blessed by having laughter play such a prominent role in my life. God's blessings were never more evident than when I recently overcame a major health crisis—lung cancer. My God-given gift for creating laughter was instrumental in helping me heal and cope with such an unexpected and uncertain life-altering situation. I never smoked, but I got lung cancer. However, I never had to ask God why, because I knew why. God apparently thought I could use some new comedy material, because it immediately occurred to me that it couldn't just be a coincidence that 'humor' rhymed with 'tumor'. Interestingly enough, I found my cancer recovery was somewhat dampened by people's reluctance to share my humorous insights into having this disease (I survived being an accountant and having cancer…cancer was easier). People just don't find cancer funny. Even my fellow comics couldn't laugh along with me. These are comics whose living is making jokes about mental retardation, AIDS, and all forms of death in general, but were uncomfortable with my cancer comedy. It's the power of cancer, the fear of cancer—it is universal and can touch anyone. It doesn't matter what race, creed, color, gender, religion, education, socio-economic level or physical condition—you are still a candidate for getting cancer. Its power can be sobering, but what everyone has to remember is to use laughter's uplifting power as the perfect counterbalance.

There are many cancer-like situations everyday waiting to metastasize in our lives. If laughter can help in enhancing your life by making you more physically, mentally, emotionally able to deal with a potentially life-threatening illness, then it can certainly aid in keeping personal, business and human relationships from becoming terminal.

I know how easy it is to become so overwhelmed by ephemeral circumstances that we can forget to laugh. Before my doctor discharged me from the hospital, after lung cancer surgery, he instructed me that I was to do nothing but lay down, rest, take it easy. The pain facilitated the acquiescence to the doctor's orders, as I was unable to do much moving around. However, I'm a hyper kind of person and even after being cut open and having a portion of my lung removed, lying down and resting, sounded more painful than sitting still. Wearing jammies and watching TV, ugh! I was losing my mind, but worse my sense of humor.

I watched games shows and found myself screaming at a contestant on the Price Is Right, for pricing a self-cleaning oven at $2,500.00. $2,500.00?!? For $2500.00 that oven better not only clean itself, but the rest of the kitchen, do some yard work and give me a sponge bath. I watched talk shows where the topic of the moment was "Who's My Baby's Daddy?" where a woman sits with a baby and nine guys who have all had to take paternity tests to see if they are the fathers of that baby. I think that the appropriate name for that show should have been "The Baby's Mama Is A Slut!" And then there were the talk shows with the "Life Coach," telling us how to live our lives—like they have the multiple personalities to be able to project specific advice into each and every one's unique life. I never saw a show with a "Laughter Coach," because at that moment, I, funny girl extraordinaire, could have used one.

It was this little foray into comedy which made me realize that even though I was not physically mobile, my mind and creativity were still free to roam. I realized I couldn't perform live comedy, but I could still find the humor in my day to day life, no matter how limited it was at the present time. So, instead of non-productive venting, I wrote humorously about any and everything that entered into my confined space. Not just jokes, but full-blown essays and they were F-U-N-N-Y! I wrote about benching "Life Coaches." I wrote about the oxy-moronic nature of the term "customer service." I wrote about how to survive a zucchini-based friendship. My comical writing was only encumbered by the frequent stops I had to make to try to catch my breath and tend to the pain in my side—not the result of the surgery, but from laughing so hard I forgot I had even had half my lung whacked off.

Laughter can be the cure for what ails you. Its effects have been proven. A doctor doesn't have to prescribe it. You don't have to pay astronomical health insurance premiums to cover the cost of it. There are no negative side effects from taking it. You don't even have to leave your home to get it. You don't have to worry about becoming drug dependent. You are the manufacturer and the ingredients are life's ups and downs. How much easier can this be? Maybe it's too easy and that's why our laughs per day are declining as we get older. We know how to work for what we want, but we seem not to know how to play for what we need. Maybe it's the lack of effective marketing. Maybe laughter should be advertised as a weight-loss program. Maybe if we could find a way to make it trendy, like water. Water wasn't valued until it was put in a bottle and sold at the store. Hopefully, it won't take some entrepreneurial, over achieving, marketing whizz to come along and put it in 16 ounce bottles and sell it for $1.39 to get people to start laughing more, but hey even at that price—laughter is a steal.

Favorite Tracks:
- Laughter heals.
- Laughter can help us handle the most difficult situations in life.
- Statistics show that people laugh less as they grow older—beat the trend!
- Inoculate yourself—find a daily dose of laughter.
- Yo Mama so skinny she could tap dance on a razor blade.

Just for laughs...

Attack Of The Fifty Foot Zucchini

Have you ever known a friend who cannot keep a house plant alive, but every year has to plant seeds for a summer garden. Always claiming that her indoor failures are due to plants needing to be outside, inhaling fresh air, growing free in a natural environment. Not "sentenced" to a life on the inside, "incarcerated" in a clay pot, unable to really stretch its roots. In her words, "A plant must be a plant, not a prisoner." She's the only person that can make her botanical ineptitude sound like a cause for Amnesty International. Yet, even outside (of those prison walls) all she can manage to grow is zucchini—nothing else. None of the other summer garden staples, tomatoes, carrots, onions, lettuce, nothing. No—nothing, except zucchini. Zucchini must be the "crabgrass" of vegetables—apparently it can grow anywhere, under any conditions, even my friend's "black thumb." The weirdest thing is she does not grow normal zucchini, like you see in the store, but colossal, mutant, killer zucchini. Every summer she has to put her furniture in storage to be able to accommodate their massive girth. She expeditiously tries to get rid of it, because it makes her a hostage in her own home. I tried to warn her—"some zucchinis need to be locked up." They're so gargantuan, they come with release papers and you have to prove to Social Services that you are qualified to give one a home. You have to complete an extensive written and oral examination to insure that you will be a fit guardian for the leviathan zucchini.

I don't really like zucchini, and year after year I remind my friend of this. Yet year after year she shows up, zucchini in tow, literally—she actually calls Triple A! It's become like a mission with her to convince others to convert their homes into halfway houses for wayward zucchini. She's always trying to sell me on the value of having zucchini in my life. Extolling all the virtues and uses of zucchini. She knows I love to cook, so she starts out by telling me all the ways zucchini can enhance my culinary experiences. "You can put it in soup, in salad, fry it, steam it, make a zucchini casserole, bake zucchini bread." After awhile she starts sounding like that character, "Bubba", in the movie "Forest Gump", when he's talking to Forest about the versatility of shrimp and therefore the anticipated profitability of going into the shrimp business. If only it was a shrimp my friend was trying to unload on me, why then I could make shrimp creole, shrimp scampi, shrimp gumbo, shrimp bisque, stuffed shrimp, curried shrimp, spicy cajun shrimp, garlic-lime shrimp, shrimp quiche, shrimp linguine, shrimp gazpacho, shrimp soufflé. You see how this problem would be solved, if only she was growing jumbo shrimp, but unfortunately it's mammoth zucchini and I'm not being enticed by her myriad of suggestions for zucchini cuisine. So, then she tries to test the validity of my epicurean credentials by saying, "If you're such a good cook, you should be able to use zucchini to create something...new, something...daring, something...extraordinary!"

When she sees I'm not jumping into that boiling pot of ego stew, desperation takes hold of her and forces her into commercial product selling mode. "You resist zucchini, yet you don't really know zucchini. You don't know of zucchini's more practical, all-purpose uses." (All-purpose uses??) "That's right, you can use the new miracle zucchini as a laundry detergent, carpet cleaner, hair shampoo, a flea collar for your dog. Use it as a paperweight, a decorative centerpiece, a flower vase, a trash compacter." (A trash compactor??) "Yes! A trash compactor! Act now and you will receive a second amazing zucchini for free!" After she's finished, in true infomercial style, a disclaimer appears (floating in midair) that says, "Results from use of this product may vary." For just a moment, I am overcome by the familiar sensation of the late night television viewing daze, where the synapses of your brain go on complete shut down and your judgment takes a leave of absence when an infomercial offers the opportunity to buy one and get a "second one free." "Free?!?" It's Pavlov ringing the bell and it starts a river flow of saliva that would challenge the most experienced white-water rafting enthusiast. Those infomercial people must be psychologists in their spare time, because that "second one free" definitely evokes the desired effect. Before that incentive is presented, that combination fishing rod/food processor/chain saw/vacuum cleaner—"for only $19.99," elicits only mild interest, but when you can get another of these invaluable multi-use contraptions for free, well that seals the deal. I don't think it's any coincidence that as soon as you hang up the phone from making that "must have" purchase, the daze dissipates and you begin returning to full consciousness, with credit card still in hand and the ink barely dry on the confirmation number etched in the palm of your hand. However, you only have a vague inkling of what has transpired, as if you were a drunk awaking from a stupor in a Motel 6 wearing only a pair of cowboy boots, with spurs, except you've never owned a pair of cowboy boots or spurs. You know something must have happened and your instincts tell you—it wasn't something good. This naked cowboy at Motel 6 image snaps me back to my present reality and gives me the resolve to resist this audacious presentation and remain steadfast in my refusal to have anything to do with the "Jolly Green Giant Zucchini."

In defense of my friend I must state that under normal circumstances she's usually not this annoyingly overbearing. During the summer she is consumed by zucchini madness and she's just not the same person. What really exacerbates the predicament and plunges her deep into this zucchini-crazed, altered reality is that she not only grows enormous zucchini, but she also grows an enormous amount of zucchini. Enough to feed all the starving people of Africa and after they've had enough (and they will), the Africans would still have enough left over to necessitate having to pawn off the excess onto the starving people in India and once they've gotten their fill (and they will), they gladly send off the remainder to the starving people of Asia and then once they tire of eating it (and they will)—they send the rest back to my friend and there she is again having to browbeat people for the sake of zucchini. It's a dilemma wrapped in an enigma. Which is somewhat redundant and quite apropos, due to the interminable adventures of the "Zucchini Chronicles." I tell her to just stop planting zucchini seeds and then no more zucchini, but she's so far gone into zucchini lunacy that she claims she no longer plants it, it just returns each summer similar to the migrating patterns that precipitate the swallows annual sojourn to San Juan Capistrano. I sense the beginning of a Vincent Van Gough level nine mental disintegration and this is the point where out of deep regard for the maintenance of my friend's sanity (and her ear), that I acquiesce and accept the vegetable monstrosities.

Now, as I sit here on my zucchini couch, my feet resting on my zucchini coffee table, with a couple of zucchini logs burning in the fireplace, sipping hot zucchini cider and eating zucchini chip cookies, I'm thinking...if life is a bowl of cherries, then friendship must be a house full of zucchini. Though,

I have to admit that this zucchini furniture is not all that bad. It's more Ikea than Drexel Heritage and there is the drawback of having to replace it every week or so, but luckily, there's ample supply of this "unique" brand of furniture just waiting to adorn someone's home and when you get a "couch," you also get a free matching "recliner." You'd have to be absolutely bonkers to pass up a deal like that...wouldn't you?

Judson Laipply

After graduating from Bowling Green State University with a Master's in Human Movement, Sport, and Leisure Studies, Judson Laipply has burst onto the speaking scene and has quickly become a breath of fresh air in a sometimes suffocating world. Creative and appealing, humorous and thought provoking, lively and enriching; these are just a few of the words that people have used to describe his style and messages.

Drawing from his vast array of experiences that include: working on a cruise ship, playing 4 years of Varsity baseball, working at a camp in Colorado, being a certified Aerobics instructor, teaching college courses, being a published poet, part-time auctioneer, and weekly columnist he can relate to almost any audience. Whether it is a specific program, or a newly designed to-meet-your-needs program, you can be sure you will be satisfied. Here are a few words from Judson:

"I always tell people how much I love what I do for two simple reasons. One, because I get to meet and work with great people all over the country, and two because I might be able to help make someone else's life a little bit better. For me there is no greater reward."

Website: www.judsonlaipply.com

The Choice is Yours

By Judson Laipply

This chapter of the book looks at recognizing your own ability to channel change; to take possession of your life and see just how much power you have over it. What I care about is helping you live the life you want and teaching you how to get it. You can create the life you want.

For years self-help authors, speakers, talk-show hosts, and others have been trying to tell us how to live a better life. Buy this book, listen to this tape, come to this seminar, and your life will be changed. Many people have tried to change their life with words of wisdom from intoxicating speakers or tear-inducing books. While many speakers have good information, much of what we hear is overused, overstated, and most of all, repetitive.

Don't get me wrong, many of the messages are important and need to be heard, but before anyone can begin to use any ideas to help make their life better, they must first understand about the power that lies within themselves. The fact is that everything changes your life. From a simple snowstorm canceling school to a death in your family—*life is change.* If you remain in a chair for one entire day doing nothing but staring out at the abyss, by the end of the day you will still be different than at the start. With your own reflection and the workings of your brain you create new thoughts, ideas, and opinions. You are constantly changing all the time. Happiness comes from knowing about change, and working to create the changes you want.

The Power of choice
The first step in any life-changing event, in any attempt to improve your life for the better, is to recognize your power of choice. Life consists of choices and consequences. Some choices are more important than others; some require more thought and energy before reaching a decision. Some take seconds to decide and others may take years, but regardless of what the choice is—it is still your choice. That is your power of choice. Before you can even think about changing your life, you have to fully embrace your

power of choice. ***Everything in your life is there because you allow it to be there through the choices you make.*** That is your power of choice, and you cannot even consider making changes in your life until you admit and validate your power of choice—know, understand, and believe that you have control over your life. Take responsibility for the choices you have made in the past and for the choices you will make in the future.

Two men were around in the days of Jesus and wanted to try and prove to the world that he was not who he claimed to be. They thought about how to discredit him, and finally came up with a plan. One day while he was preaching by the fountain they planned to catch him in a lie. They would take a tiny bird and hold it enclosed in their hand. Walking up to Jesus one of them would say, "Jesus, I have a bird in my hand—since you claim to know all—is this bird dead or alive?" Since the men were trying to catch Jesus in a lie they had it all figured out. If Jesus said that the bird was dead, the man would open his hand and the bird would fly away. If Jesus said that the bird was alive, he would crush the bird in his hand then reveal that the bird was dead. Either way they would have Jesus caught in a lie. Anticipating the joy of being right—the man asked again, "Jesus—I have a bird in my hand, is this bird dead or alive?" Jesus just looked at the man, smiled, and said—"Son, the answer to that question lies in your own hands."

The story represents how often we forget about our power of choice. We look to other people to help answer our questions for us. We seek the approval of others for what we do—we ask advice as to what we should do next, and in essence allow others to create the direction of our lives. ***Everything in your life is there because you allow it to be there through the choices you make.*** The very things you complain about are a direct result of you allowing those things in your life. Here is another story to illustrate my point—it is taken from the book *Way of the Peaceful Warrior* by Dan Milman.

Some construction workers are out on the job eating lunch one day when one of the workers opens his lunch and exclaims —"I hate ham and cheese sandwiches!" The other workers just look at him and go on eating their lunch. This goes on for several days and everyday the same story. One of the other workers is getting upset at this daily outburst so finally after hearing the man exclaim "I hate ham and cheese sandwiches" he looks over and says "Hey—why don't you just ask your wife to pack you a different sandwich?" The man gives him a puzzled look and says —"What are you talking about—I'm not married—I pack my own lunches."

Okay, so it is a little corny. I admit. Still, the point is very important and quite relevant. Ask yourself—"What am I packing in my life that I am complaining about?" What things cause you stress? Get you irritated? And how many of those things are there because of a choice you made? Complaining about the club or organization you are in? Then quit—you don't have to do it. Complaining about a boyfriend or girlfriend? Then break up with them. You see—***everything in your life is there because you allow it to be there through the choices you make.***

We feel trapped in certain situations and forget just how much power we have in our lives. The idea is that you do have a choice in every situation—this does not mean that things are going to be easy. Some choices are very hard, and we feel selfish when trying to create the life we want. Let me use the example of a boyfriend or girlfriend that you are having trouble with. You come to realize you need to get this person out of your life because they are dragging you down. You have been together for over a year, and shared many great times together, but now you realize they are not the person for you, and staying with them is only going to create misery in your life. But you feel you are betraying them by trying to get them out of you life. So rather than explain to them that you don't want any contact you allow them to stay in touch—you keep this person in your life causing you stress, heartache and pain. Why? What causes us to willingly create stress in our lives? Is it that we are compassionate, or do we fear people thinking that we are not? We don't want to hurt this other person, and that is understandable, but why hurt yourself instead? It may sound cold and inhumane, but it really is not. Once you realize that someone else is causing you pain and suffering by being in your life, you need to do all you can to get them out of your life. If you choose not to, then you have no right to complain about that person and the situation you are in. ***Everything in your life is there because you allow it to be there through the choices you make.***

The Charlie Brown Syndrome

Perhaps an easier example is one I'm sure you can relate to. In the most famous comic strip of all times, we see a perfect example of failing to see your power of choice. Remember how Lucy is always asking Charlie Brown to run and kick the football, and just as he gets close to it, she whisks it away. Charlie Brown ends up kicking empty air and lying flat on his back looking at the sky. Every time Lucy manages to convince Charlie Brown she will not pull the ball away, and like most people, Charlie knows what has happened in the past, but chooses to ignore it and the result is always the same. This is the perfect example of the power of choice. As Charlie lies on his back, feeling the pain of his last missed kick, do you think he ever said to himself "I am lying here because of the choice I made?" More likely, he is claiming—"Darn that Lucy, she is the reason that I am lying here. She pulled the ball out from me again!" Poor Charlie is not aware that most of the blame lies with him for making the same choice repeatedly.

There will be times in life when you cannot predict what will happen, when someone might purposefully pull away the football from you. This is part of life—sometimes you just don't know what is going to happen. Once you experience that situation, once you run up and kick the ball only to have Lucy pull it away, then you have an idea of what will happen. To try and make the same choice again, and expect different results, is insane. There is an old proverb that states "Fool me once—shame on you. Fool me twice—shame on me." Someone fooling you or doing something bad to you the first time—that is not your fault. To allow them in your life still, and to let them do it again—that is your fault. Does that mean people don't deserve second chances? No. You had better be careful and realize that you are the one who is giving them the second chance, and should they hurt you again, you are partly to blame because it was your choice to let them stay in your life.

Life is Change

Everything changes—nothing remains the same. As you grow, mature, develop, experience life, and reflect on your past, you are changing every minute of the day. Since everything in the world changes, **life is change.**

Think about technology and all that it offers. A little over 50 years ago, the first computer took up an entire square block. Today, there are computers smaller than the human eye that can enter a blood stream and help to combat illness and other health issues. Computer games have evolved from Atari to Nintendo to Playstation 2 and are still getting more and more realistic. Communication has come a long way; gone are the days of rotary phones and having to sit right next to the base because the cord would not reach. They have been replaced by wireless systems that allow you to roam free and make it possible to keep in touch anywhere in the world. They have even developed a receiver that can be placed in a molar tooth in your mouth and send vibrations to your ear which will be turned into the voice you want to hear—much better than holding a can with a string to your ear.

Life is not written down. Even if you are a fatalist and believe everything is already preset and happens for a reason—it is not written down. You can never know what lies around the next corner. Who you might bump into in the supermarket, what tragedy or fortune might be bestowed upon you the following day. **Life is change** and everything and every person changes every moment!

Take a look at relationships: how have they changed in your life? What do you find attractive about people today? Was it the same a year ago? Five years ago? I have kept a journal for over 10 years. At times I go back and read past entries and almost always chuckle at some of the things I have written. Many times I have been smitten by a girl and wrote something along the lines of – –"she is the one," only to see a month or so later I write—"what was I thinking?" Or times when I was sure I wanted to pursue a job or career track, and then change my mind. Humans are complex and amazing creatures and we process information all the time through all of our senses. As we take in this information we continue to change ourselves one way or the other.

As you get older, your relationships get deeper, more meaningful, and you will find they last longer as well. No doubt there are people in your life that have come and gone already—maybe you thought you would be friends forever only to grow apart after one of you moves away.

We make decisions, formulate opinions, and develop personalities, and change who we are and what we believe. All of this happens every moment of the day, and will for the rest of our lives. You are constantly changing all of the time. I cannot say this enough. **Life is change.**

As you understand and see that life is change and that you are constantly changing yourself, the questions remains, "So what?" With the knowledge of this simple concept comes the power to take advantage of the changes in your life and use your power of choice to ensure your future happiness and well being.

Formula for happiness

You understand that life is change, that people, things, and events are in a constant state of change. You should also begin to see and believe in your power of choice. If you grasp both of these concepts and truly believe in them, there is nothing to stop you from creating the life you want to live and beginning on your track to happiness. If you put the two of them together you create the perfect and simplest formula for success.

You can create the changes you want by exercising your power of choice!

Whoa... stop the presses! Did you see that? The heavens parted and this tiny light just came and shone brightly upon you right where you are standing. If you listen closely you can hear angels singing a heavenly song. Okay, maybe not, but still think about that phrase — it is pretty simple, right? An easy concept to understand, but maybe not so easy to practice. The idea is simple and the wording is plain but the actual use and practicality is another story. You have to start small and see the power you possess. Like any other concept, it takes practice and small steps to begin to create the life you want. You cannot expect to change your life overnight—you did not get to the point in your life you are now overnight did you? So let us start putting this idea into day to day practice.

You can create the changes you want by exercising your power of choice!

The First Change

Start small and create a tiny change in one aspect of your life by making a conscious choice. After this change takes place because of a choice you make, your confidence in your ability to change your life through the decisions you make will increase. Think of riding a bike for the first time, as you began to ride without training wheels, your confidence grew in your own ability to ride. Start with a small change and an easy choice and you can build confidence in your ability to take chances by exercising your power of choice.

Think about a person in your life that you are glad is there. Overall they make your life better. Choose someone you have never shared your feelings with about their importance in your life. A loved one you butt heads with from time to time or even someone with whom you always seem to be arguing. All you need to do is take the opportunity go up to that person, call, write an e-mail or letter, and say to them, "My life is better because you are in it." Any words to let that person know that you appreciate all they do for you. No, this is not some lovey-dovey, purple dinosaur mantra. This should be a heart-felt conversation where you really let the person, or people, in your life know just how much you appreciate them.

It may not be easy for you. You may feel uncomfortable. This is a normal reaction. For some reason in our society it is easier to make fun of people, point out their faults and bad habits, and do anything other than make them feel good or congratulate them on their accomplishments. In fact, most people are better at putting people down than they are at paying a simple compliment. Yet one compliment is so powerful. One heartfelt comment can bring a smile to someone's face and change the way they impact those around them. Sticks and stones can break some bones, but words can change a life.

If you consider the impact telling someone you love them or appreciate all they do for you, you would waste no time in letting those you care about know how you feel. What is holding you back? What is keeping you from looking across the table at a friend and telling them how much you enjoy their company? Maybe it is fear, maybe you think they will believe you have flipped your lid, maybe you cannot just bring yourself to say something to someone that has never been said to you. Who cares what the reason is— right now we are going to change a part of your life with this one small step.

Several years ago I had the opportunity to speak at West Point about the topic of healthy choices. During my speech I mentioned I had taught weight training and aerobics. After the program some of the football players wanted to talk about strength—how much could I bench press? I looked around the group and picked out the biggest, toughest looking person and asked, "You think you're pretty strong right?" His response was, "Yes, I am." I said "let's test your strength. I have a cell phone here. I want you to pick up the phone, dial your mother's number, and say, 'mom, I just wanted to call and tell you that I love you.'" He looked at me, thought about it for a minute, grabbed my phone and dialed. Most of his friends were in shock, surely thinking they did not have the strength of heart to do it themselves.

Here is the biggest fact of life; as you get older, beauty will fade, muscles will grow weaker, but your heart will never get smaller. Anything you can do to build your heart now will mean greater strength later in life. One way to strengthen your heart is to share your feelings of gratitude and love with those who impact your life.

Think of that one person whom you are going to tell, "I am glad you are in my life. My life is better because you are in it." Make the choice right now to do it sometime in the next three days. Make a phone call, send an e-mail, seen them face to face, or even send letter via the US postal service; whatever it is just do it. Now, make the choice to say it again to someone else. Then again, and again, and again until it becomes second nature and soon you will begin to see changes in your life. People will respect you more, want to spend time with you, and they will start to compliment you! Your life will get better. And this is just the beginning.

Make this small choice for two reasons. One, to have better relationships. Being able to compliment someone and tell them how you appreciate them is one way to create a stronger relationship. If you keep making that choice, one person at a time, it will make your life better. Two, you will see you can create changes by exercising your power of choice. If you start small and build confidence in your own abilities, you will see you can make changes through the decisions you make. You can apply this new found power into other areas of your life. Want to get in better shape? Make one choice at a time. Want to make more money? Make one choice at a time. Want to find a significant other? Make one choice at a time.

You have unlimited power to control your own happiness. Realize this amazing and fantastic ability you have and take advantage of the impact in every aspect of your life. Enjoy all that life has to offer and maximize your happiness in all things with the choices you make!

Favorite Tracks:
• Every time you complain about something or someone, think about why it or they are in your life.

• If you want to make a change in what you are complaining about, figure out what choices you must make in order to change the situation.

• Take time out of your day to compliment someone else and make his or her day better.

• Life is change, and you can create changes you want by making the needed choices.

Mary Lucas

Mary Lucas is the Assistant Dean of Students, Women's Resources and Health Education Coordinator at Kalamazoo College. She has a Masters Degree from Western Michigan University in Organizational Communication She has been active in leadership and communication training for many years, having appeared on campuses from Michigan to Florida. Her strengths lie in the areas of female/male communication, team-building and women's issues. She teaches at Western Michigan University and covers a variety of topics including communication, listening skills, conflict management, group dynamics, and interpersonal communication. Mary's enthusiasm, combined with her positive outlook and strong desire to help people understand each other better, make her a highly requested speaker.

Anne Bakker

Anne Bakker is the co-creator of the program "Becoming an Exceptional Woman." She is a speaker, agent and manager for Coleman Productions, Inc. She earned a masters degree in organizational communication, and spent more than 15 years in Student Activities both at Hope College and Grand Valley State University. After winning numerous national awards for programming excellence and graphic design, including a lifetime achievement award from the National Association of Campus Activities, her creative efforts were featured in the education section of *The New York Times*. She went on to open her own graphic design and speaking business, later teaming up with David Coleman and Coleman Productions to handle all aspects of booking, graphic design, video editing, and managing the careers of the speakers and entertainers on the Coleman Productions roster.

Becoming an Exceptional Woman

By Mary Lucas and Anne Bakker

This chapter will give you the opportunity to affirm and acknowledge the exceptional women in your life. You will begin to understand what it means to be exceptional by exploring how you can be the best you can be, what you need from others to be the best you can be, and what you bring to the group that is exceptional about you.

What does it mean to be exceptional?

Being exceptional means engaging in a process of understanding who you are as a person. It means making decisions about what you like about yourself and what you would like to change about who you are. It is the process of recognizing the positive characteristics that may be inside of you, but need to come out more often and in different ways. This is not a one-day process. This is not a one-year process. Stating "I am exceptional!" means you are committed to the lifelong process of figuring out who you are and who you want to be. Very few people take on this challenge because it is difficult, because it is a struggle, because it means finding things out about ourselves that we may not want to know. The common definition for exceptional is uncommon, extraordinary. If you are truly committed to the challenging process of understanding yourself and why you think what you think, why you do what you do, what you need from others and what you give to others, you are **un**common and you are **extra**ordinary. You are exceptional.

Appreciating The Women Who Came Before Us

Take out a pencil and a piece of paper. List the numbers 1 through 10 and set a timer for two minutes. Write down 10 women who have impacted history. Ready, go. Was this an easy exercise for you? Could you list 10? Did you list less or more than 10? Did you list people that were "famous" or people that were only famous to you?

People are often amazed at how few women we can list. It is important for us to acknowledge and learn about women who have impacted our history. These women were change-makers, and many of these women fought for the rights that we have today. If you are currently attending college, you have many women to thank. One woman that was central in fighting for the right to educate women was Emma Hart Willard. In 1818, she requested that the New York legislature allocate taxes for educating women. Although her request was denied, she later founded the Troy Female Seminary in New York, which focused on math and science and was comparable to the education men received. If you exercise your right to vote, you should know that Lucretia Mott, Elizabeth Cady Stanton, Jane Hunt, Mary McClintock, Martha Wright, and Susan B. Anthony are just a few of the women who advocated for women's right to vote. Women (and men) fought hard for the rights of women. We need to learn more about these women and share our knowledge with others. The next time you are on the internet listening to a clip from a CD you are considering purchasing, type in one of the names listed above. The next time you are instant messaging with a friend, take a break and type one of these names into your search engine. Revisit your list and post it on your wall. Keep adding to it as you learn about more and more women who had a great impact on our lives today.

Women in Your Own Life
Whom do you admire? Take some time and think about what your answers might be to this question. Can you choose 1-2 people that you admire? Now, think about why you admire those people. What qualities do they have that you admire? Take as much time as you need and really challenge yourself to think deeply about why you *admire* certain people.

Mary's Role Model
One of the people in my life that I admire is my mother. My guess is some of you will have also listed a parent or a guardian as a person you admire. My mother was the director of a shelter for victims of domestic violence for 18 years. The qualities I admire in my mother are her strength, her ability to stand up for what she believes in, her willingness to do whatever needs to be done to accomplish a task, and her commitment to a cause. A few years ago I was talking with one of my best friends and we started talking about my mom. She affirmed all of the qualities I listed above about my mom. Then she said something that caught me off-guard. She said, "and I see all of those in you, Mary." I could feel my eyes swell and I felt my face burning, both unavoidable

signs that I would soon be wearing a wet, blotchy face. People had talked to me thousands of times about the importance of role models. I read many, many books about the need to find a role model. People talk often about how my generation is suffering because we did not and still do not have strong political role models. Many people asked me the same question I asked you and I rolled my eyes and thought why do women always have to be so emotional? But on that day, talking to my friend, I got it. I understood that having role models means exactly that—I will model myself after that person. This is exactly how strong character qualities continue on in our world. I saw it in my mom and made a decision (unconscious when I was younger, conscious as I got older) that I would be like her in those specific ways. That is the best compliment I have ever received. Who do you want to be told you are just like? Who are your role models?

Consider this question that Anne asks when thinking about role models:

What do women need from each other ?
We need to feel we are not alone, that someone truly cares for us, for who we really are. While we are all truly exceptional in some way, we have a much easier time looking at other women and saying "she is exceptional because..." instead of saying "I'm exceptional because...."

It concerns me that we are unable to recognize our own treasures, while acknowledging those very treasures in others. As an exceptional women it is imperative we combat the criticism of our own selves and others. Instead, we need to spend our time examining our own self worth and celebrating the worth of those around us.

I speak to women all over the country and I see the hurt on their faces as a result of too few opportunities for them to explore and celebrate their own exceptional-ness. I recently spoke at a conference for several hundred women and when I looked into their beautiful faces I could see hope, but I also saw despair. They did not know how to affirm each other because they did not believe themselves worthy of affirmation. Answer the questions and explore with us the exceptional woman you are.

What do you need to do for yourself to be the best you can be?
We ask this question of you first intentionally. In order to be the best we can be for others, we must understand who we are and what we need to do for ourselves. All too often, we put ourselves on the back burner. One skill that is a critical element to who we are as women is our ability to recognize and be in-tune to the thoughts and feelings of those around us. This is a skill we value greatly. However, when not kept in check, we often place more emphasis on the people around us and forget about our own wants and needs. Gloria Steinem calls this, "the woman's disease of empathy sickness—knowing what other people are feeling better than we know what we are thinking" (Steinem, 1993, p. 4). This does not mean empathy has to be a sickness. It would be difficult to abandon this altogether and ignore the emotions of those around us and only focus on ourselves. This may only make us feel worse about ourselves. It does mean we need to find a healthy level of empathy and we need to balance understanding ourselves with understanding others. And so, we ask you: what do you need to do for yourself to be the best you can be? Again, challenge yourself to go beyond simplistic answers. Perhaps a few examples will assist you in thinking about your answer to this question.

Mary Reflects
The first thing I need to do for myself to be the best I can be is to stop worrying so much about what others think. This does not mean I can do or say whatever I want and not worry about how people respond to everything I say. We affect others and others affect us—we cannot separate from this. Instead this means I need to avoid worrying constantly about if I am saying the right thing and what others are thinking about me. When I do worry, I have discovered I am more anxious, more nervous and this, in turn, often makes others uncomfortable. When I decide not to worry, I am relaxed and easier to be around. I remember talking with a coworker after being in a social situation. I felt I had said something incredibly stupid (which of course I cannot remember now) to another person in the group. I told the coworker I was convinced that person was still thinking about what an idiot I was. She said to me, "do you really think people spend that much time thinking about you? That is somewhat egocentric of you. Besides, they are probably worrying about what you think of them. We worry so much about

ourselves that I don't think we have time to worry about others." It took me awhile to digest this, but once I did, I realized that she was right. If others are not worrying about everything I say, why am I?

The other thing that I need to do for myself is to laugh loudly. In high school, I had a loud laugh. I knew this laugh well; it was my mom's laugh and my grandfather's laugh. I could be at one end of the school and go to the other end and people would say to me, "I could hear you all the way from the other end of the building!" I often felt embarrassed by this and a little bit judged. Was I too loud? Was I obnoxious? Did I really want to draw all this attention to myself? Did people think that is what I wanted? Over the course of the next few years, I noticed my laugh losing its deep barreling tone. I stopped laughing loudly. I realized this a couple of years ago and have now made a conscious effort to bring back the laugh. I realized I was making a decision based on how I thought others would perceive me and I decided that was not a good enough reason to lose that part of who I am. My laugh has returned and I now work with a student who has the best (and loudest) laugh. Every time I hear her laugh, I laugh. I now see my laugh as a gift that has the power to invite others to laugh along with me. What is the one thing you have changed about yourself, maybe for the wrong reason, that you want to bring back?

What do you need from others to be the best you can be?

How often do we tell people what we need from them? How often do we do this in a constructive way? We have witnessed people forcefully telling others what they need from them. People who are forcefully told what others need often feel as if they are inadequate and the result can be a great deal of heartache and pain. Telling people what you need from them should be done in a gentle, careful way unless this person has been physically and/or emotionally abusive to you. If that is the case, you have no responsibility to communicate carefully to them. In other less serious situations, the intention is not to tell that person *who* to be, but is instead to share with them how they can assist you during a difficult time. When done carefully, everyone wins. You feel as if your needs have been met and the other person has been able to meet your needs.

In order to communicate your needs to others, you must spend time thinking about what you actually need from other people. Many students will answer this with "support" and "a listening ear." These are good answers, but think further about this. Many people need support and someone to listen to them. What need is unique to you that someone else may not know initially?

Anne Reflects

I have two women in my life who have pushed me to explore my own exceptional-ness. Every woman needs a Karen and Mary (yes, my co-author!) in their life. These two women are the ones I call when I need an honest opinion, a listening ear, or someone to laugh or cry with. I don't know how they became so significant in my life, but I know I would not be the woman I am without them. They each have a special spirit, a special gift that coupled with my own spirit and gifts make for an amazing relationship — a true friendship.

Mary's gift is her ability to challenge and support me by asking the tough questions. The questions I know need asking but I am often afraid to ask myself. She will push me in a gentle and compassionate way. She will let me talk until I have figured it out, and then ask the tough questions again to get me pointed in the right direction. The program "Becoming an Exceptional Woman" developed out of Mary's ability to challenge me with questions like how do we get women to see who they truly are? How do we get them to recognize their own exceptional-ness? Who are you? How did you get where you are? When we began to answer those questions, I began to explore my own gifts.

Karen is beautiful inside and out. Her quiet, caring spirit provides me with strength and courage when I need it most. She will always say to me, " I understand." And she truly does. She will listen to me rant and then say "I am sorry that is happening to you." Not because it has anything to do with being her fault, but she is truly empathizing with me. She shows me how much she truly cares for me in every conversation. Her style and grace are two of her best qualities. She helped me develop my own stylish look. She took me to New York and initiated me into the world of designer clothes and accessories; a world that was like being dropped into a foreign country and she was the interpreter. These trips are now a regular part of our lives and give me the ability to navigate a city like New York, and have the confidence to help others do the same.

I need both of these women in my life. They are the definition of a true friend because they are real themselves. They share who they are. They know most, if not all of my faults, but love me anyway. They let me be the real me. That is what we need most from each other —the permission to be our own true selves.

What Mary Seeks
I need someone to ask me questions until they truly understand what I am saying. Misunderstandings occur often and there is nothing we can do to eliminate them completely. However, it is important for me to know I am communicating clearly, and if I am not, I need people to ask questions so I can clarify my point. I also know I need people to truly be interested in my story. I have 2-3 people in my life who I know will always be interested in my story. I do not take many chances with my communication. I am careful who I tell what to because it is frustrating to me to tell someone who is not interested in my story. I have also decided that at this point in my life, I need someone to challenge me and point out my hypocrisies in a careful, gentle way. Yes, I will hate this at the moment, but it will help me in the long run. I need people to let me feel how I feel, even if it is not positive. Life is not always happy or easy. I need to surround myself with people who let me feel how I feel and process that and talk openly about difficult moments. Nothing is more hurtful to me than when I have spent time disclosing information to people and their response is "everything will be fine" and that is it. In the long run, I know this will be true, but at that moment, everything is not "fine" and it needs to be not "fine" at that moment in order for me to feel better later. Keep in mind that your needs will change as you get older and as your priorities change.

We encourage you to continue working on letting people know what your needs are. Have you ever been in a conversation where before you finished talking, someone started offering solutions? Here is a technique that might shift what could be a frustrating conversation to a positive interaction. Stop what you are saying and thank them for their suggestions, and then gently say, "I really do appreciate your suggestions, but I just really need you to listen right now. Could we talk about solutions in a little while?" You may be surprised at the response you get. The person might actually thank you for your honesty and they might appreciate knowing that they were being helpful just by listening.

What will you bring to your group that is exceptional about you?
Think specifically about what "group" you would like to include in this question. Maybe this is your family. Maybe it is your peer group or your student organization or your sorority. What unique and exceptional qualities will you bring to the group? How can you contribute to the success of your group?

After answering this question, many women share with us that this makes them feel uncomfortable. There are two extreme answers to this question. The first is the person who speaks very highly about herself to others on a regular basis. This is more commonly known as bragging. The other response is the person who never says anything positive about herself. There is a happy medium. Find it. Be confident about who you are, but not cocky. Be proud of who you are, but not boastful. You are a part of your "group" because you can contribute a unique aspect of who you are to that group. Utilize those strengths and be smart in utilizing the strengths of others.

How to Be Valued as a Woman:
• Be prepared to be judged.
If you have not experienced someone making assumptions about your skill level based on your gender alone, you will. This is not a complaint. This is a reality. There are many people in this world (men and women) who believe women are not as intelligent or as capable as men. You will encounter them. We encourage you to talk with other women about these experiences. Ask them if they have ever felt they were treated poorly because they are female. And if they say yes, ask them how they handled it. Listen carefully and learn from those experiences. Would you react that way? Would you react differently? What do you honestly think you would do in that situation? Preparation is key to knowing how to handle these situations in a

way that is both comfortable for you and effective.

• Be bold and confident.

Earlier in the chapter we talked about finding a comfortable, humble confidence. If you want to be respected by others, the most harmful thing you can do is to play the stereotypical, media-driven idea of the woman who obeys all the "rules" and is incapable of making her own decision. Do you ever get an immediate feeling about people based on how they carry themselves? Others will have that same experience with you. People notice how we carry ourselves within the first few minutes of the interaction. One of our favorite quotes by an unknown author is "Be bold. Even if you aren't, pretend to be. No one will know the difference."

• Force Yourself to Speak Up

All too often, women are the listeners. Similar to being empathetic, this is not a negative quality and we should appreciate our listening skills. However, sometimes we do not say enough. Our information on women and education tells us women often are not the first to speak up in classes. Women tend to think their answers through and respond. Men, on the other hand, often raise their hands quickly and will talk through their thoughts until they get to an answer. If you find you are not speaking up, ask yourself why you think this is happening. Are you intimidated by other people in class, or did you not do the reading for that day? Set a goal for yourself and start small. Perhaps your goal is that you are going to answer just one question in your afternoon class two times this week. Consider it practice. This will help you to be more comfortable speaking in all types of groups. When we speak up, it means we know that what we say *matters* and yes, what you have to say *matters.*

From Becoming Exceptional to Being Exceptional
• Recognize the impact other women have had and will have on your life.

Many women have paved the way for the opportunities we have today, and many women today continue to work for our equality. Perhaps you are one of these women. The actions of these people will have a significant impact on the rest of our lives and the lives of our younger sisters, cousins, nieces, and daughters. Recognize the little things that people around you do that have a positive impact on women and keep yourself informed about the larger societal issues. This is our role as exceptional women.

- **Have the courage to explore how you can be exceptional for yourself and others.**

Be courageous. Ask yourself the tough questions. In every situation, try to determine how you can contribute. If you leave a situation feeling as if you were not the best you could be for yourself and others, and that bothers you, reflect on that and ask yourself why. How will you handle that situation differently next time?

- **Affirm the good things people do and their willingness to take risks.**

Do you know people who never have a positive thing to say about anything? For many people, it is easier to be critical and negative than to be positive. Sometimes we can make people laugh by being critical of others. Take the high road and find other things to laugh about. Work hard to notice the good things people are doing and share that with them. Applaud them for taking chances and risks.

- **Identify the qualities in yourself that make you a role model for other women.**

Whether you want to be or not, you are a role model for other women. Ask yourself, what type of role model do I want to be? What specific behaviors do I want to role model for the others around me? This should be carefully thought out and intentional.

- **Be constructively honest in your communication.**

Honesty does not mean you say whatever you think, whenever you think it, and in whatever way you feel is appropriate at that moment. It does mean you share with people your honest thoughts and feelings in a way that does not attack their character. It does mean you share honestly because you feel it is important for others to know not to boost your own self-esteem because you have made someone else feel bad. Withholding how you really feel is dishonest. Expecting others to know or guess how you feel is unproductive. Giving yourself some time to reflect on the situation and thinking through what you are going to say before you speak is honest. Use communication constructively, not destructively.

• Take a rest from constant self-criticism of yourself and others.
Many women are overly critical of themselves and others. When an overly critical thought enters your mind about yourself, stop it. Tell yourself over and over again that you will not think that way. When you feel overly critical of others, stop and ask yourself why you are being so critical. Are you feeling jealous? Are you hurt? It is important to ask ourselves why we feel the way we feel.

• Listen to and trust your intuition.
We often forget to listen to the little voice that is leading us in a certain direction. Perhaps you have struggled to hear it. Keep listening. It will come to you when you most need it.

• Receive compliments by simply saying "thank you."
Let's practice. Here we go: It was so nice to spend this time with you! And then you say (and yes, we mean it, you should say it out loud): Thank you! Read this statement over five times and say "thank you" out loud each time. All too often we come up with lots of reasons not to accept a compliment. Work on accepting the compliment, exactly as it is.

Share Your Story
After you spend some time with this chapter, we challenge you to talk with others about your answers to some of these questions. Be confident and take a chance to share your thoughts and beliefs with other people. Share your story! Perhaps some of you will not struggle with this at all. It will be difficult for you to stop talking. Others of you may be uncomfortable talking with others. We encourage both groups to take a chance and step outside of your comfort zone. If you feel uncomfortable talking with others, step into a "sharing zone." For those of you who share often, step into your "listening zone" and utilize this as an opportunity to tell only parts of your story to encourage the other person to share their own story.

You Are Exceptional
Being exceptional does not mean you are perfect. It does not mean you will never make mistakes. It means you are real and human and that means we

all make mistakes. How will you handle those mistakes? How will you change what you are doing so you do not make the same mistake twice? I often hear students say, "oh well. I just made a mistake. We're all human." This is true, but do they ask themselves what will I do so that I don't make the same mistake twice? How will I handle this mistake? What does this say to others about who I am? We must ask ourselves those questions. We must balance realistic expectations about ourselves with never settling for being less than we know we can be.

In this chapter, we have challenged you to ask yourself these questions: what do you need to do for yourself to be the best you can be? What do you need from others to be the best you can be? What do you bring to your group that is exceptional about you? The chapter may be ending, but the challenge to ask yourself these important questions is never-ending. It is the asking and honest answering of these important questions that makes you uncommon, extraordinary, exceptional.

Favorite Tracks:
- Recognize and acknowledge the work that other people did before your time to give you the rights you have today.
- Find your humble confidence.
- Use communication constructively, not destructively.
- Bring back the laugh.
- Commit to a life-long process of understanding who you are.

Recommended Readings/Sources Used

Women's Ways of Knowing: the Development of Self, Voice, and Mind. Belenky, M., Clinchy, B., Goldberger, N., & Tarule, J. (1986). New York, NY: Basic Books.

What Every American Should Know About Women's History. Lunardini, C. (1994). Holbrook, MA: Bob Adams.

Succulent Wild Women. Sark (1997). New York, NY: Simon & Schuster.

Revolution from Within: A Book on Self-Esteem. Steinem, G. (1993). Boston, MA: Little, Brown and Company.

An extra bonus laugh track:

The Top Ten Things Only Women Understand

10.   Why it is good to have 5 pairs of black shoes.

9.   The difference between cream, ivory, and off-white.

8.   Crying can be fun.

7.   Oversized clothes, a sappy "chick flick," and a large bowl of popcorn.

6.   Why women go to the bathroom in packs.

5.   Discovering a designer dress on the clearance rack can be considered a peak life experience.

4.   The inaccuracy of every bathroom scale ever made.

3.   A salad, diet drink, and a hot fudge sundae make a balanced lunch.

2.   Why a phone call between 2 women never lasts 10 minutes.

1.   Other women!

Stephen Gray

Stephen is originally from Gloucester, Massachusetts where he lived with four sisters and two brothers (one being his twin). He graduated from Bridgewater State College, with a double major in Psychology and History and a minor in Secondary Education. He was going to teach high school until he actually taught high school. This experience sent him to graduate school where he received an MS in Counselor Education from Southern Illinois University at Edwardsville. He worked four years in the Bayous of Louisiana as a Program Advisor for the USL Ragin Cajuns. The University of Akron followed where he served as Coordinator of Student Development before putting in six years at the University of Iowa as an Assistant Director of Campus Programs and Student Activities.

Stephen teaches a Freshman seminar at East Carolina University as an Adjunct Faculty and Administrator as well as advanced leadership seminars.

Stephen has presented at many different colleges and universities across the country on topics ranging from Motivation to Group Dynamics and creating SMART Options. His programs on Greek Stereotyping have been presented at the National MGCA Conference. His program "Fire and Ice" has been presented at the International Conference of the Association of College Unions and he has presented at a number of regional conferences. His specialty is teaching common sense.

Stephen currently works as the Associate Director of Mendenhall Student Center and Director of Student Activities at East Carolina University in Greenville, North Carolina, where he lives with his wife and three handsome boys. Stephen presents the programs Becoming a Legendary Man, Creative Dating and Double Take nationwide.

"People help support what they help create!"

Becoming a Legendary Man

By Stephen James Gray

This chapter will help men come away with a better understanding of themselves and each other.

To talk about becoming a legendary man, we need to define what makes a man legendary. I looked at the men who had an impact on me and I asked why I do, or do not, see them as legendary. Was Adam, of Adam and Eve fame, legendary? Does time create the necessity to become legendary? Are famous and legendary the same? Some famous people are legendary, but why give them that status? Do historic feats necessitate legendary status? Was Hitler legendary? Martin Luther King,Jr., Jesus Christ? Are Bill Clinton, Bruce Springsteen, John F. Kennedy, Abe Lincoln, Ted Williams? All of these come to me because of their effect on history, and there are thousands more, but are they all legendary?

Are Bill Clinton, Jesus Christ, Martin Luther King, Jr., Legendary?
When you hear names such as Marilyn Manson, Bill Clinton, Jerry Springer, Martin Luther King, Jr., and Jesus Christ, what do they mean to you? If you talk with other men about these people, the topic usually comes down to "does history make the legend." Most people agree that Adolf Hitler was legendary. I want to know if it is because you know his name, or because he has impacted history. Now start thinking about accomplishments in our world. The name Bill Clinton brings out the best and worst in what people believe is right or wrong. You tell me he is legendary because of his policies that helped American society; you tell me his ethics take away that legendary status. I want to know if time is a factor in determining what makes a man legendary? In 50 years will President Clinton be remembered? Will his name be mentioned with the greats of this land? Only time will tell.

We need a place to start, and what better place than our own individual history? This chapter creates the challenge of defining what it means to become legendary. We will talk about winning and losing with grace and humility, prioritizing you morals and values, childhood memories, and barriers that prevent you from becoming the type of man you want to be. We will define class, self-control, handling success and fame, and handling failure. We will define the perfect husband, father, brother and we will also discuss the mistakes we men make.

It starts as a child. Can you remember when...
Becoming a legendary man starts at the beginning. We all have memories, some more vivid than others. The ones that stick in our mind we remember for a reason. That memory is saved for when we need it most, when we are defining ourselves as men in today's society. What memories stand out above all others, and what defines the relationship with the man or male figure that you have credited with being a positive influence in your youth? These influences are different for all individuals. Identify the one or two personality traits you feel are the best descriptors of these influential men. These thoughts and words are the standards we set to become legendary, the root and foundation of Becoming a Legendary Man.

When you decide what those traits are, recall your first childhood experience with that influential male figure. I have heard it all, from shooting their first deer at seven years old, to being cradled in their father's bosom. Some of the stories are wonderful as they display the innocence of youth while their "protector" stands watch.

One of my first memories was when my dad caught a huge Blue fish off the rocks near where we lived. I remember him carrying it up by the gills; it had to be as big, if not bigger, than I was. I was only six at the time. I remember he gutted it in the bathtub, blood and slime everywhere and my mom was not happy. It is a strange memory, but very vivid.

When I ask men to give me their scenario the majority share something positive, but some have been very blunt, such as, "He was never around and I wish I had a positive memory." Unfortunately, that is a common theme for many young men.

Take sometime to reflect on your childhood, your role model, your accomplishments and defeats, and everything society says we have to be. Childhood is the basis for the type of man we are today. Emotional memories are six times as strong, and these are talked about as the foundation of your being. What type of man do you want to be and are you preparing to be that man?

The Thrill of Victory and the Agony of Defeat

The greatest victories range from catching the winning touchdown in the state tournament, to going undefeated and pinning the #1 ranked state wrestler, to going undefeated and being pinned as the #1 wrestler. I heard someone come up with two outs in the ninth to win the state championship with a 3-run homerun. Sports are probably the biggest bond for most college-age men. I bet you could tell me where you were and who you were with when the Superbowl was played last year.

My greatest victory was being an unsung hero of sorts. I played baseball and soccer for four years at a small Division III School, Bridgewater State College. I was an OK player; I was not the best, but I was always there. I went to every practice, cheered from the bench as the younger, better players went out there on the field. I did not complain, I just kept working at it, day in and day out. Sometimes it got old, but I never wanted to give up because the team meant more to me than the personal glory. My efforts did not go unnoticed as BSC athletes of all sports selected me in my senior year to receive the "Most Outstanding Contributor to Bridgewater State College Athletics." This award is given to the athlete that goes above and beyond.

Dealing with Expectations

Part of being a man is dealing with expectations. Take a minute and write what expectations are placed on you, and who places them on you? Did you know that you as men, have to pay, have to drive, have to be the bread winners, have to be successful, have to earn and provide for your families? You have to be the best lovers, and you have to maintain an erection during intercourse for as long as it takes? You have to be mind readers, and you cannot be wrong. Oh yeah, you have to know how to get somewhere without asking for directions. That is a large list of expectations that society, family, peers, and significant others place upon you.

Is Dad Home?

The perfect Father. Ah, the irony of those words. I want you to think about what makes the perfect father. Different men come up with many similar and different things, but the number one thing that has been said by men across this country is that "in order to be a perfect father you have to be around." You have to be there, you have to be involved in our lives. All the sporting events and successes mean so much more when a "DAD" is around to witness it. Remember, you guys are not shortchanging your moms because you will always thank her whenever you are famous and on TV, but there is a special bond among men. Some other things said are, "he had to be supportive, encouraging, provide stability, be proud of the smallest things because growing up they were huge to us." Dad also has to be the provider and foundation of the family. He has to show love. Talking about love in any family will open into a wonderful conversation regarding feelings and relationships. I am talking to you about brotherhood, about dating and sex, and what she really means when she says no. She means NO.

The conversation comes full circle when you ask yourself if you are man enough to be the perfect father, brother, partner, lover. Out of all the traits we start with, creating that perfect image of what is legendary, you have to come to grips with how you are today, and are you on the right path? Think of your core values and how you were brought up. Do you live that way today? Do you treat your friends and relationships the way you were raised as a child? Your morals and values range widely but this process has started you thinking. I see men change in front of my eyes because their childhood connection to their college youth was sparking thought. Dad was home.

What holds you back from being the type of man you would like to become? Many men answer; grades, money, parents, girlfriends, abilities, and fear. A lot of you do not know if you can live up to the responsibilities of your fathers or mentors. I say you have only just begun. Dad has left the building.

The Conscience Continuum

I want you to journey through your conscience with an exercise called the "Conscience Continuum." Imagine I have placed signs up in the room that say, "Illegal," "Legal," "A Good Idea," "Not a Good Idea," "Brilliant," "Illegal but Acceptable." I will give you statements, and ask you to react and go and stand under those particular signs. You need to ask yourself why you choose to go where you go.

The first statement is "You ignore traffic signs and signals in a high crime area late at night." I have heard reactions of "Brilliant" to "Illegal but Acceptable," to "Not a Good Idea." I find these reactions depend on the region of the country I am in. You may ask what region of the country has to do with morals and values; some of the responses were based on growing up in the inner city, knowing the streets and saying "get your car out of there as fast as you can." They have seen the car-jackings, bullets shattering windows and tires blowing out. It is eye opening to hear college men talk about the realities of their world.

Next statement: "you study off of an old test, go to class, begin the test and realize it is the exact same test." This is where many men move under the Brilliant sign, yet there is always one person who says it is not a good idea. Discussion about this topic is usually pretty lively as the majority are trying to convince that one person that it is not wrong and you will get a better grade. A retort is that you are not learning, you are just copying someone else's work. What begins to emerge is something prevalent among many of today's youth, the gift of rationalization. If you can convince yourself that what you do will have no negative consequence for you, it is okay. I challenge this because there is no better, self -proclaimed rationalizer than me. I can rationalize selling matches to a firefighter, and my challenge to you is this, how do you want to be known? Is this legendary? Most will say that for this instance they are okay with it. Let's take it further: "you find a wallet with $375 in it, many credit cards and an ID. You call the person and turn back in the wallet with $325. They are thrilled to hear from you and are ecstatic."

Responses to this are very diverse. Many students rationalized that as starving college students it was okay to keep the $50 as a "finders fee." I have heard responses such as "they shouldn't have lost it in the first place," to "they had plenty." Wow. Men argued among themselves that it was okay as long as both parties were satisfied, after all, the person "was ecstatic to get the wallet back."

A true story that happened to me when I was a 15-year-old teenager. I saved up over $200 and rolled it up in my pocket and carried it down to the local Radio Shack to buy my first stereo. This was back in the day when $200 meant a great 10-watt stereo, (note the sarcasm). I was outside of the store and pulled a handkerchief out of my pocket and the wad of money fell to the ground, unbeknownst to me. I grabbed the stereo and speakers and brought them to the counter. I reached into my pocket and nothing. I searched the store, I searched outside—nothing. Needless to say that was a very traumatic episode in my life. Later that evening my twin brother, Stuart asked if I wanted to go to a party at a friend's house. I said no, but he convinced me to "get over it." I went to the party and was telling my friends the story. A parent overheard my conversation and asked me to repeat it. I did and she told me a good friend of hers was walking in front of the Radio Shack and found a bundle of money and picked it up. Not knowing what to do with it he shared this information to this person and said he would read the paper to see if anyone would put in information about the situation. Within 30 minutes this kind man was at the house and handed me a bundle of money. As a 15-year-old kid whose dream had just been shattered, another dream appeared, and this dream mattered. I offered a reward to him and all he said was that just the offer was reward enough for him.

I tell this story because it changed the way I saw things from that moment on. The generosity of people has to play a part in how we are brought up. The wallet scenario shows $50 is not going to make you rich, but it will probably carve into your morals and values. If you can personally live with that, and it's up to you, is this what you want to teach your children? Is this how your parents brought you up? Is this the act of a legendary man? These questions touch on how you are built, how you are judged. Are you a Man of Honor? Do you have class? I define class as performing a task or function the way it is intended to be performed, then taking it one step further for no other reason than that is the way it should be done. This man who returned my money was a classy man. He did something the way it should be done. He knew what it meant to have class.

I could give you more statements and have you react. Such as, you may nick a car door when opening yours and move to a different spot. You may not order the salad bar, but go up anyway. You may cash a check at a drive-thru and realize you were given $100 too much and basically say, thanks. How would you react to this scenario?

You have created the perfect father, and wrestled with that perfection not being there when you were growing up. Your moral fiber and values have been challenged, and you need to realize you are not alone. Some of you have truly questioned if what you do today reflects on your past, and if it is negative will it affect your future. This common sense factor is critical for you to realize. Yes what you do today does affect your future. One drunk-driving offense does affect the career you may want to have. One time when she said no, and you didn't think she was serious, can affect your future. Think about it.

Ten unwritten rules...
Becoming a legendary man is finding your roots and showing them in your daily lives. Think of all the legendary men that you have seen in your life. They are not perfect but there is something about them that makes you want to be "Like Mike." Take Michael Jordan for instance. To me, he is legendary and will go down in history as probably the greatest basketball player of all time. He did things we can only dream of, yet he was not perfect. He was caught in an amorous affair while married. A lot of great men and women for that matter, have faltered when it comes to maintaining a relationship. Do you judge every action the same? Do you question your own stability within relationships? These are the questions I want you to put into the back of your minds.

As you begin to reflect on your emergence as a legendary man, I want to share the **Ten Unwritten Rules Men Live By**.

Society says Thou Shall not:
- Cry (especially in public and at movies)
- Act or appear overly feminine
- Turn in another guy for anything (rat)

- Accomplish less than your father
- Be a virgin
- Be gay
- Enter an "unmanly" profession or be unemployed
- Be poor or unsuccessful
- Have only female children and not leave a namesake
- Be inept or uninterested in sports

The old saying is that "real men don't eat quiche." I say real men are not afraid to admit they eat quiche. I challenge all of these myths. You create the legend yourself.

Where do you cross the line?

The last part of our discussion is an emotional roller coaster entitled "Where would you cross the line." We cannot recreate it in writing, but imagine yourself at a "Becoming a Legendary Man" program. This is a learning tool that has no boundaries except honesty, acceptance, honor, integrity, privacy and loyalty. I ask you, for a period of about 10 minutes, to trust me and everyone in the room. You must swear to me that what is said in the room, stays in the room, and the brotherhood of legendary men will begin.

It sounds as if we are all brothers of a fraternity, a group of men bonded by the ideals and beliefs of what it takes to become Legendary. I had the privilege of doing this program for over 500 Greek men at Purdue University. This group was from all different chapters: they were mostly new members who were about to embark on their own fraternal journey. We shared something that day that will be with us for as long as we are men.

I will ask you to cross the line when I read certain statements. I challenge you that if you do not want to cross the line and it was true for you, you do not have to. I will start slowly with statements such as, how many of you were in a marching band in high school? How many of you were Homecoming King? Three sport athletes? How many were valedictorian of your senior class? (When I asked this question to the men at Purdue University, three men stood up and crossed the line. They received a standing ovation for that accomplishment. Those men did not have to do that but they felt that accomplishment deserved it.)

I will ask you about religion, beliefs in God, how many had read the entire Bible and/or Koran or other Holy Book. (Surprisingly many had done so). I will ask the Democrats to cross the line and jokingly tell you not to hit the Republicans as you walk by each other. There will be some levity in the room but this entire process is done in silence. It is an amazing thing to see, 500 plus men being quiet to finish the exercise. I ask more challenging and engaging questions. Who has been arrested, who has a tattoo, who has ever smoked marijuana, who believes in abortion, who is against premarital sex, who has parents that were divorced (almost half crossed the line). All these questions will show the similarities you have with other men.

The next question I asked and this one received the only other standing ovation, was how many were still virgins. This was where they truly crossed the line. This group of men had built up such a relationship that over 50 men crossed the line. In today's college culture not being a virgin is the status, but with these men they felt honesty was their status. I was proud of them.

Do I have what it takes?

Becoming a legendary man is a difficult, yet awesome goal. Thinking about how you were brought up, and living the right way because you choose to, is not an easy task. You are not afraid to find out who you are and honestly accept that.

Ask the question...

Here are a dozen common mistakes that men make composed by college-age men and women. Think about these as possible obstacles to becoming a legendary man.

- Men fail to follow through when they say they will. For instance, not calling back when they said they would.

- Men let romance lapse once a commitment has been made.

- Men are overly competitive, or take things too seriously.

- They let pride get in the way of common sense, such as not asking for help or directions.

- Men fail to remember details, or show interest in things that do not directly impact their life.

- Men are too success oriented and money driven at the expense of all else.

- Men try too hard to be impressive (early in the relationship) and reveal too much too soon.

- Men take on more tasks or assignments than they can successfully handle or complete.

- Men talk easily and effortlessly about topics that interest them, yet have difficulty talking about, or being interested in other things, or people.

- Men fail to form close relationships with other males, often having more female friends.

- Men fail to express themselves and their feelings openly, without being prompted, and many not even when prompted.

- Men are perfectionists to a fault.

Favorite Tracks:

• You need to be honest with yourself in order to truly find the hidden man inside.

• You need to find the strength that childhood gives you. Learn from your defeats and cherish your victories.

• You need to care about other men; you have many things in common.

• You need to keep on the road to becoming legendary, and be the classy individual you know you can be.

Coleman Productions represents informative and entertaining speakers, specializing in motivational, leadership, orientation and retreat programs. Our goal is to educate while we entertain and be the company you want to work with again and again. Our motto is...Timely Topics. Great Speakers. Life Changing Results. We hope after working with us you'll agree. Our goal is to accommodate your needs, meet your budgetary restrictions and provide you with an act or program that will leave your audience buzzing.

For more information about one of the speakers featured in *Leadership's Greatest Hits* contact:

Anne Bakker
Agent/Manager
Coleman Productions, Inc.
616-392-8943
www.colemanproductions.com